The Caine Prize for African Writing 2012

African Violet
and other stories

The Caine Prize for African Writing 2012

African Violet
and other stories

New Internationalist

The Caine Prize for African Writing 2012

First published in 2012 in Europe, North America and Australasia by
New Internationalist™ Publications Ltd
Oxford OX4 1BW
www.newint.org
New Internationalist is a registered trademark.

First published in 2012 in Ghana by Sub-Saharan Publishers
P.O. Box 358
Legon-Accra
Ghana
www.sub-saharan.com

First published in 2012
in Southern Africa by
Jacana Media (Pty) Ltd
10 Orange Street
Sunnyside
Auckland Park 2092
South Africa
www.jacana.co.za

Cover design by Publicide.

Design by New Internationalist.

Printed in Hungary.

British Library Cataloguing-in-Publication Data.
A catalogue record for this book is available from the British Library.

Library of Congress Cataloguing-in-Publication Data.
A catalogue record for this book is available from the Library of Congress.

New Internationalist ISBN 978-1-78026-074-7
Jacana ISBN 978-1-4314-0492-6
Sub-Saharan Publishers ISBN 978-9988-647-96-4

Contents

Introduction

My first year as Administrator has featured a great deal of change at the Caine Prize. In April we appointed the internationally acclaimed Nigerian writer Ben Okri as our Vice-President and deputy editor of *Granta* magazine, Ellah Allfrey, became our new Deputy Chairperson. We are committed to making Caine Prize stories available to read on the continent, so we are delighted that this year we have agreed co-publishing arrangements with three more African publishers. FEMRITE in Uganda, Sub-Saharan Publishers in Ghana and Bookworld Publishers in Zambia join the long-standing partnerships we already have with Jacana Media in South Africa, Cassava Republic in Nigeria and last year's addition of Kwani? in Kenya. We have also added to the website substantially and created a blog as well as developed our Facebook and Twitter presence. And finally we have developed a partnership with the literacy NGO Worldreader to make the first nine award-winning stories available free to African readers via an app on their mobile phones.

Selected from 122 stories from 14 African countries, this anthology contains the stories from the 13th annual Caine Prize shortlist, along with those from our 10th workshop for African writers which was held in South Africa earlier in the year. Stanley Kenani was shortlisted in 2008 and Billy Kahora received an honourable mention in 2007. For the first time the Chair of Judges summarized the shortlist as showing 'the range of African fiction beyond the more stereotypical narratives. These stories have an originality and facility with language that made them stand out. We've chosen a bravely provocative homosexual story set in Malawi; a Nigerian soldier fighting in the Burma Campaign of World War Two; a hardboiled *noir* tale involving a disembodied leg; a drunk young Kenyan who outwits his irate employers; and the tension between Senegalese siblings over migration and family responsibility.'

This year's shortlist has already garnered press interest, and was the subject of 'A Blagger's Guide' in the *Independent on Sunday* on 6 May 2012, in which it was dubbed 'The No 1 African Short Story Competition'. The 2012 shortlist comprises:

- Rotimi Babatunde (Nigeria) 'Bombay's Republic' from *Mirabilia Review*, Vol 3.9 (Lagos, 2011) http://mirabilia.webs.com/
- Billy Kahora (Kenya) 'Urban Zoning' from *McSweeney's*, Vol. 37 (San Francisco, 2011) www.mcsweeneys.net
- Stanley Kenani (Malawi) 'Love on Trial' from *For Honour and Other Stories*, published by eKhaya/Random House Struik (Cape Town, 2011) www.randomstruik.co.za
- Melissa Tandiwe Myambo (Zimbabwe) 'La Salle de Départ' from *Prick of the Spindle*, Vol 4.2 (New Orleans, June 2010) www.prickofthespindle.com
- Constance Myburgh (South Africa) 'Hunter Emmanuel' from *Jungle Jim*, Issue 6, (Cape Town, 2011) www.junglejim.org

The winner will be decided by a panel of judges chaired by author and Fellow of the Royal Society of Literature Bernardine Evaristo. Joining her are: award-winning cultural journalist Maya Jaggi; Zimbabwean poet, songwriter and writer Chirikure Chirikure; Associate Professor at Georgetown University Samantha Pinto; and the award-winning CNN television correspondent Nima Elbagir. As has been the case in recent years, the winner will be invited to undertake a residency at Georgetown University at the Lanaan Center for Poetics and Social Practice. We also intend to consolidate invitations to take part in events at the Open Book Festival in Cape Town and the Museum of African Art in New York.

This year's workshop took place at Volmoed, in the Valley of Heaven and Earth (*Hemel en Aarde*), near Hermanus in South Africa. We are greatly indebted to Bernhard Turkstra for hosting us with such warmth and generosity and to Marie Philip who, amongst many other things, helped us to find Volmoed. The 10 workshop participants from six different African countries were guided by the celebrated writers Henrietta Rose-Innes (South Africa) and Jamal Mahjoub (Sudan). Two Nigerian writers were unable to join us, despite our best efforts, due to unresolved visa and immigration issues between the South African and Nigerian governments.

The principal sponsors of the 2012 Prize were the Oppenheimer Memorial Trust, the Booker Prize Foundation, Weatherly International plc, China Africa Resources plc and Miles Morland. The British Council also gave valuable support, and Kenya Airways and the Beit Trust both provided travel grants for workshop participants. There were other generous private donations, and vital help in kind was given by: the Royal Over-Seas League; Bodley's Librarian; the Rector of Exeter College, Oxford; the Royal African Society; Jacqueline Auma of the London Afro-Caribbean Book Group; Tricia Wombell, Coordinator of the Black Reading Group and Black Book News; the Southbank Centre; Nii Parkes at African Writers' Evening; the School of Oriental and African Studies; Kings College London; and the Institute of English Studies, University of London. We are immensely grateful for all this help, most of which has been given regularly over the past years and without which the Caine Prize would not be Africa's leading literary award. I believe this year's shortlist and the workshop stories contained in this anthology represent the best of African short fiction published in 2012.

Lizzy Attree
Administrator of the Caine Prize for African Writing

Caine Prize 2012
Shortlisted Stories

Bombay's Republic

Rotimi Babatunde

THE OLD JAILHOUSE ON THE HILLTOP had remained uninhabited for many decades, through the construction of the town's first grammar school and the beginning of house-to-house harassment from the affliction called sanitary inspectors, through the laying of the railway tracks by navvies who likewise succeeded in laying pregnancies in the bellies of several lovestruck girls, but fortunes changed for the building with the return of Colour Sergeant Bombay, the veteran who went off with the recruitment officers to Hitler's War as a man and came back a spotted leopard.

Before Bombay's departure, when everything in the world was locked in its individual box, he could not have believed such metamorphosis was possible. A man was still a man and a leopard a leopard while the old jailhouse was a forsaken place not fit for human habitation. A white man was the District Officer who went by in an impressive white jacket and a black man was the Native Police constable who saluted as the white man passed. This was how the world was and there was no reason to think it could be otherwise. But the war came and the bombs started falling, shattering things out of their imprisonment in boxes and jumbling them without logic into a protean mishmash. Without warning, everything became possible.

✻✻✻

Months preceding the arrival of the military bands, news had been filtering in that the foreign powers were clawing at each other's throats. In the papers, there were cartoons showing how bad things would be if Hitler won. Posters appeared all over town encouraging the young men to enlist and then the recruitment officers showed up accompanied by drum majors who conducted smartly uniformed bands through the streets. Unmoved by the marching songs and colourful banners flying above the parades, not a single volunteer stepped out. Shrugging, people just said, the gecko and the lizard may decide to get married, fine for them, but it would be silly for the butterfly to dance its garments to shreds at their wedding celebration. The next day, traditional drums accompanied the bands to rouse enthusiasm but this also failed to inspire and speculations became rife that conscription would be used as in some other places. But that was not to be because reports came that Hitler himself was waiting with his ruthless army at the border and that with him things were going to be much worse than the imagination could conceive. Those he didn't pressgang into slavery would be roasted alive for consumption by his beloved dogs, this was the word on the street, and panic began spreading with virulent haste.

There was only one thing to do. Hitler had to be taken on before he overran their homeland, so the young men began enlisting in droves. Among them was Colour Sergeant Bombay. He would quickly find out that someone must have confused his nation's domestic frontiers with a place half the world away. The only terrain on which he would war was 44 days and several bouts of seasickness from his homeland by ship, in an alien jungle where, after two years of nightmarish combat as part of the Forgotten Army, he would be stunned by the realization that everything he thought fantastic was indeed credible.

* * *

When the bugle sounded and Bombay woke with a jerk in the darkness, he didn't know where he was or what on earth he was doing there. The space in which he found himself was too large to be his bedroom. Its array of double bunks stretching away into the dimness was spooky in the waning moonlight and the shrouded figures rousing on the bunks seemed like creatures materializing out of a bad dream. The bugle sounded once more and it all came flooding back to Bombay, the long lorry ride from his hometown with the other recruits and the thickness of the dust on their bodies and, on arrival at the camp, the granite face of the warrant officer who supervised the distribution of kits to the lost-looking recruits. Bombay's joints still ached from the rattling of the wooden floorboard where he had sat, cramped with his colleagues in the lorry's rear like livestock huddling together for warmth. He didn't wait for the third and final bugle before jumping down from his bed. That was the beginning of his first day at training camp.

He went mechanically through the warm-up exercises and completed the arduous challenge of the roadwork. After a quick breakfast, he stood ramrod stiff as the drill sergeant moved between the files barking instructions. Later that day, with his muscles sore and his head throbbing from the day's long exertions, it suddenly struck him that he liked it. Everything in military life was clear and ordered. That was what he wanted and he found nothing more satisfactory.

At dinner time, listening to the recruits drawn from distant places on the continent speaking a plethora of languages he did not know existed, Bombay marvelled at his superior officers' ability to whip that Babel with just a few commands into a single martial unit. As he continued eating, the polyglot buzz of impenetrable speech swirled on around the dining hall without unleashing bedlam, contrary to what Bombay would have predicted. There are many things I know nothing of in this world, Bombay exhaled as he shovelled another spoonful of barracks mess into his mouth. Things he never knew were possible.

* * *

Bombay had to like Ceylon, if only because it provided an escape from the nausea. In the weeks at sea, he had vomited so much he would have loved any land, but the coconut-dotted beaches of Ceylon and the bullock carts plodding down the lanes and the monkeys that sneaked into their base to dash off with whatever was not secured made Bombay's fondness for the island easier.

The recruits had completed their basic training before setting sail. On disembarking, they began preparations for jungle combat. Their base was in a village just outside Colombo. The training at the village was good. As the recruits jogged past, the women picking leaves in the tea estates would stop to look. Every evening a cart brought down containers of coconut wine for the soldiers to drink and, sometimes, Bombay dared the local gin that tasted fierier than gasoline.

Bombay did not mind that the baths were segregated, one for the African soldiers and another for the Europeans. The village headman often came around when the men were bathing. As the days went by, the crowd that came with him grew larger. The visitors always headed straight to scrutinize the Africans as they washed but never bothered to check out the lathering Europeans. It was then Bombay became puzzled about what was going on. He made enquiries and was assured that the villagers meant no harm. Reports had come that the pants of the African soldiers were sewn three-quarter length to conceal their tails and the headman was bringing his villagers to confirm if this was the case. Bombay was not angry. He simply found it interesting people could assume he had a tail. The chance of anyone having such a belief was something he had not considered possible.

* * *

Bombay's discoveries of the possible would come faster than the leeches in Burma's crepuscular jungles. At first, Bombay's tasks were limited to mule driving and porting baggage. If there are people trying to kill me, it would be stupid of me not to be in a position to kill them also, he repeatedly grumbled to his superiors. To shut him up, he was posted to a combat unit.

The campaign to recapture Buthidaung was in progress. Bombay's unit was deployed to a swampy pass of the Kaladan Valley where they got isolated from the main army for weeks. Their situation got dire and it seemed they would have to feed on wild bananas lined with pawpaw-like seeds but tasting like detergent. Then Bombay's squad ran into enemy ambush. They had no option but to dive for cover as hostile gunfire reduced the vegetation above their heads to shreds. Their ammunitions had already gone too low to mount a credible resistance but Bombay thought it wiser to go down fighting and his squad agreed. They charged shrieking at the machinegun position with pangas raised, their common howling and bawling coming as if from a primeval horde of lunatics hell-bent on murder. The firing stopped. Perhaps a freakish mistake damaged the enemy's equipment mid-operation, anyone would have assumed. When the manic charge Bombay led reached its destination, the enemy was gone. The squad met three machineguns and several abandoned magazines, the operators of the weapons long melted into the greenery like frost crystals blown into the jungle's humid oven. To Bombay's astonishment, all the firearms were in excellent working condition. The captured guns ensured the squad's return to base. On arrival Bombay was made a lance corporal, the first of the promotions that would elevate him to the rank of sergeant and carrier of the regimental flag, and given the Distinguished Conduct Medal for bravery, one of the three medals he would be awarded on the front.

Shortly before the decoration ceremony, Bombay protested to his Lieutenant that he had taken his action not because of bravery but out of fear, and deserved no honour for valour. The officer smiled. That was the first time Bombay had seen him grinning. Oh poor you, so you don't even know why the Japs fled, the Lieutenant said. The stories that preceded you to this war said that the Africans are coming and that they eat people. We fuelled those rumours by dropping leaflets on the enemy, warning them that you will not only kill them but you also will happily cook them for supper. The Japanese, as you very well know, are trained to fight without fear of death. They don't mind being killed but, like anyone else, they are not in any way eager to be eaten. Their training didn't prepare them for that. That was why they scrammed when they saw you screaming towards them like bloodthirsty savages. But anyway, that you know nothing about the situation only makes your action more courageous. Report in an hour to receive your decoration. Okay?

Bombay saluted. The normally stern-faced Lieutenant, recalling the incident, was tickled out of his reserve. He started chuckling as he walked away, finding the comedy of the engagement with the Japanese so hilarious that tears streamed down his cheeks as he burst into outright laughter. He contemplated the emotions experienced by the Japanese soldiers as Bombay's squad bore down on them and the terror that must have gripped the enemy on concluding it was a clan of cannibals from Henry Rider Haggard's gory tales making a sortie for lunch. His laughter was still sounding a minute later when he made his entrance into the canteen, desiring to calm the mirthful paroxysms rocking him with a drink.

In the Lieutenant's wake, Bombay stood perplexed for a long spell, trying to come to grips with the revelation he had just received. Perhaps human flesh may be prime-grade meat but he had never imagined eating anyone for a meal or even as a quick snack. Thinking more about it, Bombay's stomach got queasy and he had to steady his rising urge to puke. That people would imagine he was a cannibal was something he had not thought was possible.

✳ ✳ ✳

Bombay would never hear the Lieutenant laugh again. Some weeks after Bombay's decoration, the Lieutenant's unit was separated from the division by blazing howitzers during a large push to drive the Japanese out of the winding road leading to Kalewa. Before nightfall, everyone in the group was accounted for except the Lieutenant.

Bombay admired the officer despite his mirthless countenance. The tactics he deployed when he led a tricky assault on a troublesome hilltop battery had struck Bombay as brilliant and, in those anxious moments only a cigarette could relieve, the man did not need to be asked before offering his last half-stick to whoever needed it the most. Oftentimes he had sat late with Bombay, sharing stories about his childhood on a farm bordered by a tiny lake near the Cumbrian Mountains and lamenting how much he missed the mooing of the cows when they were being led back from grazing in the unpredictable fog. This was why Bombay was happy to be included in the party tasked with finding the missing officer.

It was a dangerous mission. The more tenacious pockets of enemy combatants were still booby-trapping the jungle. The captain who led the search had recently arrived from Europe at the front. The men complained about his dismissive bossiness and the way he bragged about himself as if he was the special one sent to conclude the war singlehandedly. Someone once wondered why a man who could not even relate well with his own people was given charge over soldiers from a continent whose cultures he knew nothing about. Bombay, though, never griped about things like that. The front had been a good teacher to him. He was confident that the captain, by the time he ceased being a sophomore under the jungle's tutelage, would learn that life and war were more complex than the textbooks he had read in the military academy.

The lessons provided by the search expedition would be brutal on the new officer. It was the height of the monsoon and, for weeks, the rains had been coming down with pestilential resolve. The search was just beginning when the downpour became even more oppressive. The dampness was no longer news. Squelching around in soggy boots and dripping fatigues was a constant drudge they endured with amphibious fortitude, and the men found the captain's continuous bitching about the weather irritating. He stopped talking when they came upon a mound of charred enemy corpses in a ditch which served as a gun pit. Their burns were clearly not from grenades or kindred explosives. The corpses had been incinerated by their vanquishers with flame throwers to prevent disease. Executing such cremations had long become routine for Bombay. The mission moved on.

Dim shards of light constituted all the brightness able to breach the vegetation canopy. In the half-dark, having to beat new paths through the undergrowth was a thankless chore. Far more vicious than the stinging nettles and topping the jungle's sundry tortures was the omnipresent menace of the tiger leeches. The bloodsuckers were like fair punishment on both sides for their collaborative orgy of mass slaughter.

Since the encounter with the immolated bodies, the captain had been in increasing distress. His condition worsened after the party chanced on one of their soldiers who had fallen into an enemy poison pit. No one could say if he had bled to death from gashes inflicted by the sharp bamboo spikes or if he had succumbed to blood poisoning from the rotten meat with which the spikes were laced. From his advanced state of decomposition, it was evident he had been there for a while. The group advanced after retrieving the soldier's name tag and noting the location. By then, the captain had become a liability to the expedition. His constant lagging behind was hampering the group's progress and his unbroken whimpering and jabbering was only tolerated because the muffling drone of the rain made it a manageable risk. The next ranking officer had taken de facto command and, with night rapidly approaching, he was thinking of calling off the search mission when the flashlights of Bombay and his colleagues picked up a figure. The man was stripped stark naked and tied to a tree, as if on death row awaiting his executioners. It was the missing Lieutenant. He was dead but there was no sign that he had been shot. His body had been severally pierced. The spectacle of his entrails spilling out of his excavated stomach and drooling down to his toes could not have been ghastlier. Bombay winced. The pain eternally howling from the Lieutenant's frozen face left no doubt that he had been used as bayonet practice by his enemy captors while still alive.

Confronted by that horror, the captain's visage turned ashen. It seemed his dilating eyes would soon pop out of their sockets. His breathing deteriorated into a sharp gasping for air, as if from lungs compromised by pneumonic failure. Then the captain began weeping, slobbering for his dead mother to emerge from her grave and save her innocent son from the Japanese and the gluttonous leeches, to take him away from the monstrous labyrinth of the jungle because he had no idea what he was doing there and how to get himself out of it. The oblivious blankness of his eyes confirmed that something had snapped. The captain's own volition could not sustain him on his feet. Two soldiers on either side had to support him back to base.

Over the next few days, the captain's condition deteriorated. He stayed in bed all day, shivering and whimpering. Everything terrified him, including daylight, and he kept his face shrouded with a blanket. The stench reeking from him became overpowering because the bed which he never left also served him as toilet, and at night he was always sedated because of fears his impromptu yelling could provide bearings to troops attacking in the darkness.

The captain's dead mother did not come over to spirit him away from the jungle, possibly from a dread counterpart to her son's for the enemy's eviscerating bayonets. Instead, it was a single-engine Moth that could only evacuate one patient at a time which finally flew him to a psychiatric hospital. Bombay was deeply shocked by the captain's fate. He remembered the white-jacketed District Officer back home with his manicured nails and the imperious airs of one in absolute control of the cosmos, the white man oozing superiority over the khaki-clad Native Police constables as if merely exercising his natural birthright. That the captain, a countryman of the colonial administrator, had disintegrated to a condition that pitiful meant the impeccable District Officer could likewise descend to the same animal depths. Bombay had seen a lot in the war. Diarrhoeic Europeans pestered by irreverent flies while the men shat like domestic livestock in the open. Blue eyes rolling in mortal fear as another enemy shell whistled past. But never before had he imagined one of his imperial masters degenerating into a state so wretched. He found it good to know that was also possible.

✳ ✳ ✳

Bombay's universe of the feasible continued expanding with inflationary acceleration. Buthidaung was successfully occupied and his division advanced down the Mayu Valley, manoeuvring into position as part of the pincer movement to prevent the Japanese escaping through the Kaladan corridor. In the Mayu basin, Bombay's platoon had to traverse an extensive stretch of elephant grass. The plants were especially tall and their leaves slashed like a field of razors, lacerating the face and making progress on foot through their scarifying gauntlet interminable. In the middle of that grassy stretch, the platoon came upon corpses from a friendly battalion. The European cadavers were left whole but the African ones had been chopped up.

The Japs are convinced black soldiers resurrect, said an officer, so they dice the corpses to forestall having to kill them twice.

Bombay was incredulous. You mean... they believe it is possible we rise up to continue fighting them after we are killed? he asked.

Yes, the officer replied, chuckling.

Every one of us?

Yes.

Just like Lazarus?

Why?

And like Jesus Christ, your saviour?

A scowl had replaced the smile on the officer's lips. Yes, he said.

In the silence afterwards, the only sound came from the rustling of the elephant grass. I could not have reckoned anyone would think black people can rise from the dead, Bombay thought. He would never forget that. The platoon moved on.

✳ ✳ ✳

At Bombay's new base, a bombardier was grounded after roughing up a fellow airman competing with him for the attentions of a pretty military nurse. The affections of the nurse belonged to his rival but the bombardier still carried her picture, like an ancestral amulet, in his wallet. He had to be restrained within a makeshift stockade when his unrequited passion spiked up his aggressiveness.

A few days into his confinement, the bombardier broke out in the small hours and overpowered the soldier guarding the corral. Bombay was standing as sentry outside the barracks that night. The manic bombardier had killed one man and injured another three with the Bren gun he seized from his guard before Bombay shot him. Once. The bombardier died on the spot.

Afterwards, smoking as daylight began reddening the east, Bombay remembered his countryman Okonkwo, whose story would become famous some years after the war when it was told in a book titled *Things Fall Apart*. Decades before, Okonkwo had killed an arrogant constable of the new colonizers. To deprive the white men of the pleasure of doing the same to him, Okonkwo hanged himself. Yes, those Bombay had been killing in the war were of a lighter hue than he was but they were not white men and, even then, their killing had been sanctioned by his imperial overlords. Now, Bombay had killed a white man, not the black servant of the white man or the alien antagonists of Europe. Bombay vowed to take the brave route of Okonkwo rather than having anyone lead him to the gallows.

The next day, Bombay received a letter from his commanding officer. To Bombay's shock, it commended Bombay for his quick thinking, which had prevented a bigger carnage from decimating the barracks.

* * *

So Bombay was surprised to know it was possible to be praised for killing a white man, as he would also be astounded in the Kabaw Valley on observing that the Japanese snipers were still resolute in their refusal to target his side's stretcher bearers. This was the same enemy who not only slaughtered their opponent's wounded in captured hospitals but also shot their own injured men if they lacked the resources to evacuate them during hasty withdrawals, yet here they were still refusing to shoot at their opponent's stretcher carriers. Bombay shook his head in confusion, lost in bewilderment, as he would the evening his platoon leader told him that a strategic bridge over a tributary of the River Irrawaddy no longer needed to be taken.

What about the enemy soldiers on the other side? Bombay asked.

We no longer have any enemy on the other side, the platoon leader said.

They were still shooting only a short while ago.

Yes, but we no longer have any enemy on the other side.

Bombay could not get it but he shrugged off his befuddlement. If they are gone, that means we will soon be going to Malaya, he said. People are saying we will soon be invading Malaya since there is not much fight going on here any more.

We won't be going anywhere.

Bombay noticed that the platoon leader looked unusually exhausted. What is happening? Bombay asked, his apprehension mounting.

Nothing. The war is already over, you know. Nothing will be happening except our respective journeys home, the platoon leader replied.

The big bomb had sprouted its mushrooms over a week before. The documents of surrender were already signed but news of the ceasefire was slow in getting to the troops who, in their ignorance, were still fighting on days after the war had been declared ended.

We have won the godforsaken war, said the platoon leader, without any euphoria. The only place we are going now is home.

Considering both men's downcast looks, they might as well have lost. Along with the crudity, the war had brought along its own kindergarten certainty, kill or be killed, and the confirmation of its end brought no joy, only difficulty in comprehending the sudden evaporation of the matter which had dominated their recent years. On arrival at the front, Bombay like every other soldier was buoyed by the deluded faith that, unlike those dying around him, he would survive the enemy's bullets. With time such thoughts went extinct and the only things he bothered about were pragmatic routines, like drying out his wet boots and getting his gun loaded and enduring the fangs of the ever-thirsty tiger leeches. In that robotic existence, Bombay had no luxury to indulge in speculations about victory or defeat. Now, the war was over. To his surprise, he was still alive and he had to begin thinking of the return journey home which only minutes earlier was so remote it wasn't a practical possibility.

We should begin packing our bags, Bombay said.

Yes.

The platoon leader began walking away and then he turned back to Bombay.

On your way home don't worry about what you will tell your loved ones or your friends about the part we played in this war, the platoon leader said. No-one will know where you were and, if you try informing them, they will not know where this is. We call this the Forgotten Front and we call ourselves the Forgotten Army. That is the lie we flatter ourselves with. I tell you, this is not the Forgotten Front and we are not the Forgotten Army. Nobody has ever heard of us so they can't even begin forgetting about us. That is the plain truth. To the world, we might never have existed.

The platoon leader, a no-nonsense combatant from the Welsh highlands, was almost in tears as he pondered the destiny of their common struggle on that neglected front, an effort that, true to his prophecy, would remain anonymous, like the travails of faceless and nameless characters forever entombed in a book of fiction that will never be written. The platoon leader plodded away with heavy steps, his spirit sapped to the lees by his valedictory agonies.

Bombay watched him go. He sighed. Bombay didn't care much about memory or forgetting. For him, things would never be locked in boxes again and that consciousness, the irreversible awareness handed out not by charity to Bombay but appropriated by him from the jungle without gratitude and by right, was enough recompense from the war. With the campaign over, the only thing that mattered to Bombay was the brand-new universe of possibilities he would be taking home with him from the front.

* * *

Politics was pungent in the air when Bombay returned to his homeland. The nationalist leaders had gotten more clamorous in their criticism of the colonialists and there were editorials in the dissident newspapers denouncing the big bomb's deployment as racist because it wouldn't have been dropped on Europeans. The atmosphere was spiced up by the evening assemblies under the acacia tree near the market. Having discovered the necessities of parliamentary representation and the right to self-rule during their travels, the brightest of the veterans freshly returned from Burma zealously quoted Gandhi and Du Bois at incendiary gatherings which constables from the Native Police Authority oftentimes had to break up.

Much was expected of the veteran who had distinguished himself above the lot by receiving not only the Distinguished Conduct Medal and the George Cross but also the rarely awarded Victoria Cross for conspicuous bravery. People were disappointed, though, because Colour Sergeant Bombay showed not the slightest interest in populist agitation. The taciturn man seemed content strutting around in his blue PT gear and staring with unseeing blankness through the eyes of anyone who looked in his direction. Whenever grownups asked him if the Japanese were really as brutal as the other veterans reported, Bombay would reply with one of his newfound cryptic sentences. We did them no harm and they did us no harm, he would say, we only tried to kill each other as often as we could. And when people pressed him further to say something concrete about the war and his Japanese enemies he would truncate the discussion by saying, the white man dropped the big bomb on them but they are talking with each other now. They were good friends before and they are back as good friends again.

It became obvious Bombay was more comfortable chatting with the younger ones. He spoke to them of the tiger leeches and the horror that surges through the body at the instant you feel their fangs sinking into you, the discharged Sergeant schooling the wide-eyed children about how the leeches must not be plucked out because they leave their fangs behind and, instead, should be scorched off with a match or lighter since burn marks are kinder on the skin than the sepsis festered by their abandoned fangs. He exposed his torso and the children saw the dark stains singed by the flames all over his skin, like rosettes on a leopard's coat. This is the story of how I became a spotted leopard, he said, and his juvenile audience gleefully sprang back in mock fright when he snarled at them like the feline beast.

He got the name which replaced his original one from the tales he told about Bombay. The city was called Bombay because its streets were littered with bombs through which pedestrians must carefully tiptoe, the veteran said, except if one fancied levitating sky high as blown-up mincemeat.

The youngsters had overhead their teachers speaking in school about the Black Hole of Calcutta. They asked Bombay if he came across the hole during his sojourn abroad and the man replied, Of course. Bombay described the sinister darkness of the abyss into which, after dropping a coin, you could wait for all eternity without the shadow of an echo returning from the fathomless deep. That is why it is called the Black Hole of Calcutta, the veteran said. When sheep fell into the hole, an occurrence whose regularity wasn't surprising since they were the most foolish creatures alive, continued Bombay, the sheep tumbled for days on end down the Black Hole of Calcutta which ran straight through the centre of the earth but he assured his enraptured listeners that, luckily for the foolish sheep, their owners always found the dazed animals grazing happily on the other side of the globe close to where they popped out of the pitch-black shaft.

The children were pleased to hear him narrate his barehanded battles with the crocodiles lurking beneath the muddy waters of the Irrawaddy, the veteran whispering to them that the females had gold nuggets for eyes and the males stared coldly at the world with fist-sized diamonds which, if plucked from their sockets, would be sold for an amount large enough to make the wealthiest man around seem the most miserable pauper.

The story the kids requested he repeat over and over was the one about the clan of weeping jinni who followed him for seven days and seven nights through the jungle pleading to buy his rare African soul with the most fabulous riches this world has to offer. A bit envious of the attention Bombay was giving the youngsters, some grown-ups made mockery that, considering the strange light burning in Bombay's eyes, it was not impossible that the veteran, as substitute to his three-medalled soul, had bartered off a slice of his sanity to the desperate creatures.

Wit morphed into reality when confirmation came that Bombay had taken possession of the long-empty jailhouse, disregarding the accounts of ghosts and dreadful presences which had long kept everyone away from the building. On the day of housewarming, Colour Sergeant Bombay lowered the imperial flag in his new residence and proceeded to declare his person and his house thenceforth independent from the British Empire. That action got many people wondering if the ravenous leeches Bombay moaned so much about had not sucked his head hollow during the jungle war, siphoning out his brains and leaving behind only the most idiotic dregs for him to bring home to Africa.

✳ ✳ ✳

The morning the tax collectors visited the old jailhouse, Bombay was drinking from a large gourd of palm wine and puffing a cigarette on the landing attached to the upper floor. In front of the building, a flag with a spotted leopard leaping in its centre fluttered its sedition in place of the colonial banner whose deposition by Bombay had been the high point of his eccentric housewarming ceremony. The newest free nation of the world, this was how the veteran referred to his newly inaugurated People's Republic of Bombay.

Near the mast, rough-hewn busts commemorated the founding fathers of the infant republic. The figures increased in scale from the first to the last, concretizing Bombay's perception of their order of importance. Major General 'Fluffy' Ffolkes, Commander of Bombay's Division in Burma. Lieutenant General Slim, Commander of all the Divisions of the Forgotten Army. Lord Louis Mountbatten, Supreme Commander over the Allied Armies in the eastern theatre. And, finally, triumphant at the apogee of that evolution as if he was the Seal of the Generals, stood the bust of Colour Sergeant Bombay, pioneer President and Commander in Chief of the newborn Republic of Bombay.

The visiting tax collectors interrupted their progress towards the veteran's residence to read the names etched below the figures, bemused by the cheekiness of the iconography informing Bombay's diminutive Mount Rushmore Memorial. They were still laughing at the veteran's impudence when they reached the staircase winding up to the upper floor of the old jailhouse. Bombay had been watching them all along, panting with rage as the visiting bureaucrats jabbed their fingers in ridicule at his ancestral totems. The collectors were surprised when they looked up to see Bombay standing right above them. They greeted him. He didn't reply. After some seconds, he spoke. Did you collect the necessary visas?

The taxmen were stumped.

Are you deaf? I said did any of you collect a visa before crossing the border?

We are tax collectors. Bring out your tax receipt.

Bombay got angry. This is an independent republic, he thundered. And get this into your rotten heads, this nation is not part of your bloody Commonwealth and it will never join. You and your children will always need visas to enter here. Next time you trespass into this territory, you will be shot dead. Like the enemy spies you all are. Every one of you. Is that clear?

The threat of gunfire brought about nervous movements from the taxmen. Their leader, who was accustomed to being dreaded rather than confronted, tried to assert his authority as delicately as he could. We simply came here to do our job, he said. We are not here to make trouble but if you give us trouble then we will be forced to give you trouble in return.

Is it that clown, Charles, who sent you here?

Charles? We were not sent by any Charles. We are tax collectors. The District Officer would be annoyed if we report you to him. Of course, you would not want that to happen, would you?

Ah, the District Officer. The goat is called Charles. Isn't that his name?

You are calling DO, the white man... like any name.... that he is a goat. The DO is the DO. You are looking for big trouble, said the scandalized team leader.

Charles is the name his father gave him, so let him use it. From today on you must call him by his first name, Charles, not DO. Is that clear?

Bombay had threatened to shoot. In the silence, the uneasy tax collectors kept an alert eye on the wine-guzzling veteran looming over them like murder. They fidgeted with anxiety about where the situation was heading.

Call him what you like and we will call him what we like, one of them mustered the courage to say. But please tell us, have you paid your hut tax? We are here to collect your hut tax. If you don't co-operate, we will call the Native Police and they will take you straight to prison.

Bombay laughed. Tell Charles that this is a big building built of stone. It is not a hut and it is much larger than that useless house he lives in, wasting his evenings planting flowers that can't grow in this weather and rearing cats like a white witch.

How dare you come here asking for something as ridiculous as my hut tax? It is a shame that, in your slumber, you all choose to point your empty heads in a single direction. If your employer Charles is a blind fool, are you all also dumb that you can't tell him this is not a hut but a free and independent republic which he has no right to invade?

But that wasn't really the point, the collectors were explaining when Bombay stormed in, banging the door on their explanations that the tax was necessary for the smooth running of the colony.

The taxmen were discussing their next course of action when Bombay came out dressed in full ceremonial uniform, the Victoria Cross glistening in concert with the other medals dangling around his neck. He bellowed at the officials and demanded to know where they were when, after crossing the River Chindwin, ten men from his division died drinking from a lake the enemy had poisoned. He asked them what they were doing when his superior officers told him not to take his pants off as he washed in a stream so as not to frighten people with the exposure of his monkey tail. Still screaming with fury at the taxmen, Bombay asked if Charles, the stupid fellow who calls himself the District Officer, knew anything about Kabaw where, in the Valley of Death, tiger leeches descended on his platoon like an ambush of assassins and if any of them, arrogant white master or cringing black servants, will ever in their petty lives visit Rangoon where a full General decorated him with one of the many medals around his neck while, resplendent, a military band trumpeted its exultation. Then Bombay stopped talking. He fiddled with his trousers and began roaring a Gurkha song whose lyrics were in a language none of the collectors could understand.

Later, in the report they gave the District Office on their return to Colony House, the tax collectors would admit that they thought Bombay had exhausted his mulishness and was making to bring out his hut tax from his trouser pockets so they were caught unawares when the veteran's penis popped out instead and urine began jetting down at them like a waterfall from above. Being bathed in excrement is a taboo in our culture, they would note, so we had to scamper back from the disgusting horror sprinkling towards our heads.

They ran even faster when the first gunshot sounded. The taxmen, who on the evidence of that day might have made a good career for themselves as Olympic sprinters, were already at the compound's gate when the second shot came. A good distance from the building, the only one among the collectors who had the courage to glance back saw the golden liquid still shooting out of Bombay's fly, the endless torrent fed by the gallons of palm wine the man had been imbibing since daybreak.

The District Officer pondered over the incident for several days. Bombay was adamant in his refusal to pay his tax and he had scared away representatives of the Crown so he deserved to be arrested. An utterly contemptible cad, this was how the District Officer described Bombay. The colonial administrator, though, was not so naive as to conclude that the resolution could be so simple. He regretted Bombay's possession of firearms, which complicated the issue. Yes, there were enough arms-bearing Native Police constables to execute a successful storming of the old jailhouse, but the veteran was a screwball with sufficient knowledge of warfare to mount a stiff and suicidal resistance from his hilltop position, an engagement that could also be fatal to a good number of the constables. An Empire-tired MP could take interest in the affair and, notwithstanding the fact that Bombay was no more than another native conscript, the rebellious veteran could become a poster boy for the Empire's detractors, held up by the home country's troublemakers because of his status as a multiply decorated war hero. The District Officer did not fancy having to defend the slaughter of such a person at the Foreign Office or in Parliament. Involvement in a messy situation like that could very well be it for his career.

To worsen the scenario, the native firebrands campaigning for independence could latch on to the matter as a fulcrum on which to hinge their campaign. It was that final realization that clinched the District Officer's decision for him. Better let sleeping dogs lie, he reasoned. Bombay was like a disease which had quarantined itself. There was nothing smarter than letting him be, if only to guarantee his disconnection from wider political activity, the District Officer resolved, grudgingly allowing Bombay an independence whose legitimacy the veteran could not recognize because he had long before then unilaterally imposed the same upon himself.

***

The District Officer's reasoning proved sound. Bombay stayed away from the nationalist agitators, devoting his efforts instead to drafting a 792-page constitution for his hilltop republic and sending communiqués to the world press about the first general elections in the domain which, inevitably, returned the enclave's sole citizen as President.

Many years after Bombay's renegade republic was inaugurated, the colonial flag descended for the last time in the veteran's abandoned nation. Bombay wrote to his counterpart in his nation of birth, congratulating him on the belated independence and promising that Bombay's older republic would be glad to volunteer wisdom to the rookie state whenever necessary. The letter was never acknowledged but that rebuff only fired President Bombay's resolve.

He wrote endless letters to the heads of state of the newly independent nations of Africa and granted interviews to any pressman who wanted one. Soon, people began paying attention. Impressed by his credentials as a war hero and intrigued by his rhetoric, national leaders from all over Africa invited him to grace ceremonies in their countries. Bombay called these trips state visits. He always reminded his hosts that giving your guest something good to take away, if possible cash, was a venerable African tradition so he never returned empty-handed from his trips. Whenever there was a coup or a regime change, Bombay's Republic was one of the first to grant recognition to the new government. In appreciation, more gifts came Bombay's way and the GDP of his republic kept up a healthy annual growth.

The longer he stayed in power, the more Colour Sergeant Bombay found it necessary to give himself ever more colourful titles. Lord of All Flora and Fauna. Scourge of the British Empire. Celestial Guardian of the Sun, Moon and Stars. Sole Discoverer of the Grand Unified Theorem. Patriarch of the United States of Africa. Chief Commander of the Order of the Sahara Desert and the Atlantic Ocean. Father of the Internet. When Bombay ventured out of his hilltop republic, it was in a convoy of siren-blaring vehicles as interminable as those of the rulers he hobnobbed with during his continent-wide trips, and he always flew into a rage if anyone failed to address him as His Excellency, President of the People's Republic of Bombay, followed by a listing of his titles which were so numerous that not even Bombay could remember them all.

Bombay would rewrite his republic's constitution 11 times and serve as the enclave's President for 47 arbitrary tenures after elections won with landslide support from his republic's sole citizen, himself, until death finally unseated him from office.

The obituary, titled 'Bombay's Republic', penned by a columnist working for a newspaper published in Bombay's birth country, would have pleased the veteran. Colour Sergeant Bombay, war hero and perpetual president, was loved without exception by all the citizens of his People's Republic of Bombay, so ended the tribute. No-one argued with the claim since it was only natural for a person to love himself without reservations.

Before Hitler's War spawned possibilities in his universe like body bags on the Burma front, Colour Sergeant Bombay would not have believed an obituary so affecting could come from a newspaper based in a country he considered foreign.

Rotimi Babatunde's stories and poems have been published online and in print. His plays have been broadcast on the BBC World Service and performed at venues including Riksteatern, the Royal Court Theatre and Halcyon Theatre. He is the recipient of a Ludwig Vogelstein Foundation fiction grant and a fellow of the MacDowell Colony, Ledig House and the Bellagio Centre, among others. He lives in Ibadan, Nigeria.

Urban Zoning

Billy Kahora

OUTSIDE ON TOM MBOYA STREET, Kandle realized that he
was truly in the Zone. The Zone was the calm, breathless place
he found himself in after drinking for a minimum of three
days straight. He had slept for less than 15 hours, in strategic
naps, had eaten just enough to avoid going crazy, and had
drunk enough water to make a cow go belly-up. The two-
hour baths of Hell's Gate hot-spring heat had also helped.

Kandle had discovered the Zone when he was 17. He had
swapped vices by taking up alcohol after the pleasures of
casual sex had waned. In a city-village rumour circuit full of
outlandish tales of ministers' sons who drove Benzes with
trunks full of cash, of a character called Jimmy X who was
unbeaten in about 500 bar fights going back to the late '80s;
in a place where 60-year-old tycoons bedded teenagers and
kept their panties as souvenirs; in a town where the daughter
of one of Kenya's richest businessmen held parties that
were so exclusive that Janet Jackson had flown down for her
birthday – Kandle, self-styled master of The Art of 72-Hour
Drinking, had achieved a footnote.

In many of the younger watering holes in Nairobi's CBD,
he was now an icon. Respected in Buruburu, in Westlands, in
Kile, in Loresho and Ridgeways, one of the last men standing
in alcohol-related accidents and suicides. He had different
names in different postal codes. In Zanze he was the Small-
Package Millionaire. His crew was credited with bringing
back life to the City Centre. In Buru he was simply Kan. In the
Hurlingham area he was known as The Candle. In a few years,

the generation of his kid brother Giant Rat would usurp his legendary status, but now it was his time.

The threat of rain had turned Tom Mboya Street into a bedlam of blaring car horns, screaming hawkers, screeching *matatus* and shouting policemen. People argued over parking spaces and haggled over underwear. Thunder rumbled and drowned it all. A wet wind blew, announcing a surreptitious seven-minute drenching, but everybody ran as if a heavy downpour threatened. Even that was enough to create a five-hour traffic jam into the night. The calm and the wise walked into the bars, knowing it would take hours to get home anyway.

Zanze patrons walking into Kenya Cinema Plaza shouted jeers at Kandle because he was going in the opposite direction, out into the weather. Few could tell he had been drinking since noon. Kandle was not only a master at achieving the Zone, he was excellent at hiding it. The copious amount of alcohol in his blood had turned his light-brown skin brighter, yellow and numb and characterless like a three-month-old baby's. The half bottle of Insto eyedrops he had used in the bathroom had started to take effect. He had learned over time that the sun was an absolute no-no when it came to achieving a smooth transition to the Zone. Thankfully, there was very little sunshine left outside, and he felt great.

'Step into the p.m. Live the art of 72 hours. I'm easy like Sunday morning,' he muttered toward the friendly insults. A philosopher of the Kenyan calendar, Kandle associated all months of the year with different colours and hues in his head. August he saw as bright yellow, a time when the year had turned a corner; responsibilities would be left behind or pushed to the next January, a white month. March was purple-blue. December was red. The yellow haze of August would be better if he was to be fired from his job at Eagle Bank that evening.

Kandle had tried to convert many of his friends to the pleasures of the Zone, with disastrous results. Kevo, his best friend, had once made a deep cut into his palm on the dawn of a green Easter morning in Naivasha after they had been drinking for almost a week. He had been trying to impress the crew and nearly bled to death. They had had to cut their holiday short and drive to Nairobi when his hand had swollen up with infection days later. Kandle's cousin Alan had died two years ago trying to do the 50-kilometre Thika–Nairobi highway in 15 minutes. Susan, once the late Alan's girlfriend, then Kandle's, and now having something with Kevo, stopped trying to get into the Zone when she realized she couldn't resist stripping in public after the 72-hour treatment. After almost being raped at a house party she had gone into a suicidal depression for weeks and emerged with razor cuts all over her body and 20 kilograms off her once-attractive frame.

Every month she did her Big Cry for Alan, then invariably slept with Kandle till he tired of her and she moved on to Kevo. The Zone was clearly not for those who lacked restraint.

Stripping in public, cutting one's palm, thinking you were Knight Rider – these were, to Kandle, examples of letting the Bad Zone overwhelm you. One had to keep the alcohol levels intact to stay in the Good Zone, where one was allowed all the wishful thinking in one's miserable life. The Bad Zone was the place of all fears, worries, hatreds and anxieties.

Starting off toward Harambee Avenue, Kandle wobbled suddenly, halting the crazy laughter in his chest. Looking around, he felt the standard paranoia of the Zone start to come on. Walking in downtown Nairobi at rush hour was an art even when sober. Drunk, it was like playing rugby in a moving bus on a *murram* country road. Kandle forced himself back into the Good Zone by going back to Lenana School in his mind. Best of all, he went back to rugby-memory land, to the Mother of All Rugby Fields, Stirlings, the field where he had played with an abandoned joy. He had been the fastest player on the pitch, a hundred metres in 12 seconds easy, ducking and weaving, avoiding the clueless masses, the thumbless hoi polloi, and going for the girl watching from the sidelines. In his mind's eye the girl was always the same: the Limara advert girl. Thin and slender. Dark because he was light, slightly taller than him. The field was next to the school's dairy farm, so there were dung-beetle helicopters in the air to avoid and mines of cow-dung to evade.

He could almost smell the Limara girl and glory a few steps away when a Friesian cow appeared in the try box. It chewed cud with its eye firmly on him, unblinking, and as Kandle tried to get back into the Good Zone he saw the whole world reflected in that large eye. The girl faded away. Kandle put the ball down, walked over to the cow, patted her, and with his touch noticed that she was not Friesian but a white cow with some black spots, rather than the other way around. The black spot that came over her back was a map of Kenya. She was a goddamn Zebu. All this time she never stopped chewing. With the ball in the try box he took his five points.

Coming back to, he realized he was at the end of Tom Mboya Street. A fat woman came at him from the corner of Harambee Avenue, and just when she imagined that their shoulders would crash into each other Kandle twitched and the woman found empty space. Kandle grimaced as she smiled at him fleetingly, at his suit. At the corner, his heightened sense of smell (from the alcohol) detected a small, disgusting whiff of sweat, of day-old used tea bags. He stopped, carefully inched up against the wall, calculated where the nearest supermarket was, cupped his palm in front of his mouth, and breathed lightly. He was grateful to smell the toothpaste he had swallowed in the Zanze toilets. The whiff of sweat was not his. That was when Kevo came up to him.

'Fucking African,' Kandle said. 'What time is it?'

'Sorry we were late, man. Here's everything. Susan's upstairs. We just got in and Onyi told us you'd left.'

'I'm starting to lose that loving feeling for you guys,' Kandle said, taking the heavy brown envelope from Kevo, who began doing a little jig right there on the street, for no sane reason, jumping side to side with both feet held together. Passersby watched with amusement.

'Everything else was sent to Personnel,' Kevo said, still breathless. 'So good luck.'

'Were you kids fucking? That's why you were late?' Kandle grinned, seeing that the envelope held everything he needed.

Kevo smiled back. 'See you in a bit.'

As they were parting ways, Kevo shouted to him.

'Hey, by the way, Jamo died last weekend. Crashed and burned. They were coming from a rave in some barn. Taking Dagoretti Corner at 8 a.m. at 160 – they met a *mjengo* truck coming from Kawangware. Don't even know why they were going in that direction. Motherfucker was from Karen.'

'Which Jamo?'

'Jamo Karen.'

Kandle rolled his eyes. 'There are about five Jamo Karens.'

'Jamo Breweries. Dad used to be GM.'

'Don't think I know him.'

'You do. We were at his place a month ago. Big bash. You disappeared with his sis. Susan was mad.'

'Ha,' Kandle said.

'Anyway, service in Karen. Burial in Muranga. Hear there are some wicked places out there. Change of scene. We could check out Danny and the Thika crew. You know Thika chicks, man.'

'I'll think about it.'

'You look good, baby,' Kevo said, and waved him off.

Kandle suddenly realized that he had forgotten his bag. It meant he was missing his deep-brown stylish cardigan, his collared white shirt, his grey checked pants, his tie. He should have asked Kevo to pick it up for him. Feeling tired, he almost went under again.

Since childhood, Kandle had always hated physical contact. This feeling became especially extreme when he'd been drinking. It had been worsened by an incident in high school – boarding school. One morning he'd woken up groggily, thinking it was time for pre-dawn rugby practice, and noticed that his pyjamas were down around his knees. He was hard. There were figures in the dark, already in half-states of readiness, preparing for the 12-kilometre morning run. Nobody seemed to notice him. He yanked his smelly shorts on, and while his head cleared he remembered something.

Clutching hands, a dark face. He never found out who had woken him up that morning, and after that he couldn't help feeling a murderous rage when he looked at the faces in the scrum around him, thinking one of them had abused him.

Over the next few months, during practices, he looked for something in the smiling, straining boyish faces, for a look of recognition – he couldn't even say the word 'homosexual' at the time. With that incident he came to look at rugby askance, to look at Lenana's traditions with a deep, abiding hatred. Then one day he stopped liking the feeling of fitness, the great camaraderie of the field, and started feeling filled with hate when even the most innocent of tacklers brushed by him. He took to cruelty, taking his hand to those in junior classes. He focused on his schoolwork, became supercilious and, maybe because of that, ever cleverer, dismissive of everyone apart from two others who he felt had intellects superior to his. He became cruel and cold. His mouth folded into a snarl.

In spite of a natural quickness, he'd never succeeded in becoming a great rugby player. Rugby, he discovered, was not for those who abhorred contact. You could never really play well if you hated getting close. Same with life and the street, in the city – you needed to be natural with those close to you. As he went up Harambee Avenue, he realized he was well into the Bad Zone. Looking at his reflection in shop windows, he felt like smashing his own face in. And then, like a jack-in-the-box that never went away, his father's dark visage appeared in his mind's eye, as ugly as sin. He wondered whether the man was really his father.

After completing third form he had dropped rugby and effaced the memory of those clutching hands on his balls with a concentrated horniness. He became a regular visitor to Riruta, looking for peri-urban pussy. One day, during the school holidays when he was still in form three, he had walked into his room and found Atieno, the maid, trying on his jeans. They were only halfway up, her dress lifted and exposing her thighs. The rest of those holidays were spent on top of Atieno. He would never forget her cries of 'Maiyo! Maiyo! Maiyo!' carrying throughout the house. God! God! God! After that he approached sex with a manic single-mindedness. It wasn't hard. Girls considered him cute. When he came back home again in December, Atieno wasn't there; instead there was an older, motherly Kikuyu woman, ugly as sin. His father took him aside and informed him that he would be getting circumcised in a week's time. He also handed him some condoms.

'Let's have no more babies,' was all he said after that.

On Harambee Avenue, three girls wearing some kind of airline uniform came toward him in a swish of dresses, laughing easily. He ignored their faces and watched their hips. One of the girls looked boldly at him, and then, perhaps for the first time that day, a half-stagger made him realize how drunk he actually was, though it would have been hard for anyone apart from his father to tell.

And so the Bad Zone passed on. He quickly fished into his jacket pocket and came out with a small bottle of Smirnoff Red Label vodka, swigged, and returned fully to the Good Zone. Ahead of him was Eagle Bank. He smiled to himself. He forced himself to calm down and breathe in. The usually friendly night watchman, Ochieng, was frosty.

'You are being waited for,' he said in Kiswahili, shaking his head at the absurdity of youth.

Inside he was met by the manager's secretary, Mrs Maina, a dark, busty and jolly woman. She too was all business today.

'You are late, Kandle,' she said. 'We have to wait for the others to reconvene.'

This was the first time she had ever spoken to him in English. She had lost that loving Kikuyu feeling for him.

Kandle, who knew how to ingratiate himself with women of a certain age, had once brought Mrs Maina bananas and cow innards mixed with fried *nundu*, cow hump, for her birthday. She had told him later that they were the tastiest things she had ever eaten, better than all the cards she'd received for her birthday. Even the manager, Guka, coming out of his office and trying some, commented that he wished his wife could cook like that.

Mrs Maina blurted out another few words as Kandle waited outside the manager's office. She sounded overcome with exasperation.

'What? What do you want? Do you think you're too good for the bank?'

'No. I don't want much. I think I want to become a chef.'

She couldn't help it. They both laughed. Kandle excused himself and went to the bathroom.

When he was alone he removed a white envelope from his jacket pocket and counted the money inside again. Sixty thousand shillings, which he planned to hand over to the accountant to pay for the furniture loan he had taken out before he went on leave. Back in the bank, Mrs Maina told him that the committee was ready, and Kandle was ushered into Guka's office.

There was a huge bank balance sheet in the centre of the desk. Guka Wambugu, the branch manager, was scowling at the figures. The man was dressed like a gentleman farmer, in his perennial tweed jacket with patches at the elbow and a dull, metallic-grey sweater underneath, over a brown tie and a white shirt. All he needed were gumboots to complete the picture. Kandle noticed that the old fool wore scuffed Bata Prefect shoes. Bata Mshenzi. Shenzi type. Kandle held down the laughter that threatened to burst out of his chest.

Some room had been created on each side of the desk for the rest of the committee. Mr Ocuotho, the branch accountant, sat on Guka's right, looking dapper and subservient as usual, his face thin and defined, just shy of 50 and optional retirement. He was famous in the branch for suits that hung on his shoulders like they would on a coat hanger. He was a cost-cutter, the man who stalked the bank floors like a secretary bird, imagining the day he would have his own branch to run. He had once been the most senior accountant at the largest Eagle branch in Kenya, and had been demoted to the smaller Harambee branch only after a series of frauds occurred under his watch. As a result, though he was here representing the bank's management, he was partly sympathetic to the boy in front of him. He had been in the same position, albeit at a managerial level.

Next to Ocuotho, at the far-right corner of the desk, was a bald-headed man, Mr Malasi, from Head Office Personnel. He was wearing designer non-prescription spectacles. Kandle thought he recognized him from somewhere. At the far left, representing the union and, in theory, Kandle, was the shop steward, Mr Kimani, a young-looking, lanky, 40-year-old man with curly hair and long, thin hands that he cracked and flexed continually. He also happened to be Kandle's immediate boss.

He was the man behind the year-long deals in the department. On Kimani's right was a younger man, the deputy shop steward at the branch, Mr Koigi, a rounded youth with a round belly and hips that belied his industry. He had had an accident as a child, and was given to tilting his head to the right like a small bird at the most unlikely moments. Like Kandle, he had worked at the bank for a year, and was considered a rising star. He was also Kandle's drinking buddy.

There was a seat right in front of the desk for Kandle. Just as he was lowering himself into it, sirens blared, and everyone in the room turned to watch the presidential motorcade sweep past, out on the street. The man, done for the day, heading home to the State House. Kandle grinned, and remembered shaking the President's hand once when he was in primary school, as part of the National Primary School Milk Project promotion. There was an old photo of Kandle drinking from a small packet of milk while the President beamed at him. The image had been circulated nationwide, and even now people stopped Kandle on the street, mistaking him for the Blueband Boy, another kid who had been a perpetual favourite in 1980s TV ads.

When the noise died down, Guka turned to him.

'Ah, Mr Karoki. Kandle Kabogo Karoki. After keeping us waiting you have finally allowed us the pleasure of your company. I am sure you know everybody here, apart from Mr Malasi, from Personnel.' Guka stretched his arm toward the bald-headed man in the non-prescription spectacles. His back was highly arched, as usual; his eyes were those of an old tribal elder who brooked no nonsense from errant boys. Kandle suddenly remembered who the bald-headed man was. He was the recruiter who had endorsed him when he had first applied for his job.

Guka turned to the shop steward. 'Mr Kimani, this committee was convened to review Mr Karoki's conduct, and to make a decision – sorry, a recommendation – to Head Office Personnel.' He gave Kandle a long, meaningful look. 'This is not a complex matter. Mr Karoki decided he was no longer interested in working for Eagle, and stopped coming to work. Before me, I have his attendance record, which has of course deteriorated over the last two months. Prior to this, Mr Karoki was an exemplary employee. We have tried, since this trend began, to find out what was wrong, but Mr Karoki has not been forthcoming. What can anyone say? I am here to run this branch office, and eventually, as the Americans say, something has to give.' He paused, cleared his throat, and looked out the window with self-importance. Then he turned back to Kandle.

'The British, whom I worked for when I joined the bank, would have said Queen and Country come first. Eagle next. At that time, when I joined, I was a messenger. The only African employee at Eagle. I worked for a branch manager named Mr Purkiss, a former DC who made me proud and taught me the meaning of duty. I have been here for 40 years. I turn 60 next year. It seems that young men no longer know what they are doing. When I was your age, Mr Karoki, no one my age would have called me Mister. I was Malasi's age, 36, before anyone gave me a chance to work in Foreign Exchange. I was already a man, a father of three children. Now look at you. You could have been in my seat, God forbid, at 40. It is a pity that I did not notice you before this, to straighten you out.' He paused again. 'But before we hear from you, let us hear from the branch accountant, Mr Ocuotho.'

By now everyone from the branch was trying to hide a smile. Mr Malasi had a slight frown on his face.

'Thank you, Mr Guka,' Ocuotho said, clearing the chuckle from his throat. He spoke briskly.

'Mr Karoki is a good worker, or was a good worker. But after he received his June salary, which was heavily supplemented by the furniture loan he took, he never came back. We received a letter from a Dr Koinange, saying that Mr Karoki needed a week off for stress-related reasons. After that week, he did not appear at work again. This is the first time I am seeing him.'

Mr Malasi shifted in his seat at the mention of Dr Koinange. Kandle was looking at his boss, Kimani, who wore a grave expression. Feeling Kandle's eyes on him, he made the most imperceptible of winks.

'What was the exact date of this doctor's letter?' Guka asked. Everyone waited as Ocuotho referred to his diary.

'Friday, 24 June.'

'Today is Thursday the 15th of August. So not counting his sick and annual leave, Mr Karoki has been away for two weeks with no probable reason. And after eight weeks, he doesn't seem to have solved his problem.' Mr Malasi coughed, but Guka ignored him. The manager stretched and stroked his belly. 'Let us hear from the shop steward, Mr Kimani.'

Kimani straightened up. 'I have worked with Kandle for a year,' he said, 'and in all honesty have seen few hardworking boys of his age. A few weeks ago he failed to appear at work, as Mr Ocuotho has mentioned. He called in later and said he wasn't feeling very well, and that something had happened to his mother. He said he would be sending a doctor's letter later in the day. I didn't think much of it. People fall sick. Kandle had never missed a day of work before that. I told him to get it to the accountant, give the department a copy, and keep one for himself. Then, of course, he went on leave. When he didn't come back as scheduled – I was to go on leave after him – I got worried and tried to get in touch. When we spoke, he told me his problems weren't done and that he claimed to have talked to Personnel. I told him to make sure that he kept copies of his letters.'

Mr Guka was getting agitated. It was obvious he was not aware of any contact with Personnel, with whom he'd already had problems. After he had accused the legendary Hendrix of insubordination, Personnel had decided otherwise and transferred the man to Merchant Services, which was a promotion. Hendrix was now Eagle's main broker. Guka had been branch manager for eight years; his old colleagues were now executive managers or had moved on to senior positions at other companies.

Guka loosened his tie. He remembered that he was due to retire at the end of the year. He wished he was on the golf course, or out on his tea farm, and reminded himself that he needed to talk to Kimani later, to find out whether there was any chance that the currency deals would start up again. It had been two months since he had received his customary 20,000 shillings a week. He needed to complete the house he was building in Limuru. This was not going the way he had expected.

'I am not aware of any such documents or communication,'

Mr Malasi offered. 'But as you all know, we are a large department. It's certainly possible we overlooked something. I will check up on that.'

Guka cleared his throat. 'I think the facts are clear –'

Malasi interrupted him. 'I think we should hear from Mr Karoki before we decide what the facts are.' Head Office Personnel had paid out millions of shillings to ex-employees for wrongful dismissal, and Malasi was starting to wish he had stayed away from this one and sent someone else. It was looking like one of those litigious affairs. For one, the boy seemed too calm, almost sleepy. And what was the large sheaf of documents he had in his lap? The reference to one of Nairobi's most prominent psychiatrists, Dr Koinange, had introduced a whole new element.

Dr Koinange happened to be on Eagle Bank's board of directors. The belligerent hubris of one old manager would be, in the face of such odds, ridiculous to indulge. Even if they managed to dismiss the boy, Malasi decided he would pass on word that Mr Guka should be quietly retired. As the oldest manager at Eagle, he was well past his sell-by date. Malasi decided he would recommend Ocuotho as a possible replacement.

Guka cleared his throat again. 'Young Mr Karoki, you have five minutes to explain your conduct.' His easy confidence had become a tight and wiry anger. 'Before you start, maybe we should address the small matter of the furniture loan you took out.'

Kandle quietly removed the white envelope from his pocket and placed the shillings, together with the contents of the large brown envelope, on Mr Guka's desk.

Malasi reached for the documents and handed copies to everyone. Kandle spoke in a quiet voice.

'Over the last year, my mother has lost her mind. Being the first-born, with my father's constant absences, it has been up to me to look after her. My sister is in the US, and my brother lives in a bottle. Two months ago my mother left my father's house in Buruburu and moved to a nearby slum. At the same time, I started to get severe headaches. I could not eat or sleep, and even started hallucinating, as Dr Koinange, our family doctor, explains in one of these letters. He has expressly told me that he would be in touch with the bank's personnel department. That is why I haven't been in touch. My doctor has.' There were tears in Kandle's eyes.

Guka sat back in his seat and glared at the ceiling. He tucked his top lip into the bottom, re-enacting the thinking Kikuyu man's pose. The Kikuyu Lip Curl.

Malasi looked up from the documents. It was time to end this, he thought.

'Yes, I can see that Personnel received letters from your doctor. I also see there are letters here sent to us from your lawyer. Why go to such lengths if you were truly sick?'

'I thought about resigning, because I did not see myself coming back to work unless my mother got better. But my lawyer advised that that wasn't necessary.'

One tear made it down his left cheek. Kandle wiped it away angrily.

'Do you still want to resign?' Malasi asked, somewhat hopefully.

'I'd like to know my options first.'

'Well, it won't be necessary to bring in your lawyer. No. It won't be necessary. We will review your case and get back to you. In the meantime, get some rest. And you can keep the money, the loan, for now. You are still an employee of this bank.'

He turned to everybody. 'Mr Guka?'

The manager glared at Kandle with a small smile on his face. He remained quiet.

'Mr Karoki, you are free to leave,' Mr Malasi said.

As they all trooped out, leaving Mr Guka and Mr Malasi in the office, Kandle realized that he had just completed one of the greatest performances of his young life.

He hummed Bob Marley's 'Crazy Baldhead' and saw himself back in Zanze till the early hours of the morning.

'Can I see you for a minute in my office?'

It was Ocuotho. Before Kandle followed him down the hall, he shook Kimani's and Koigi's hands and whispered, 'I'll be at Zanze later.' Then he walked after Ocuotho, into the glass-partitioned office right in the middle of the bank floor.

'Why didn't you tell me about your problems?' Ocuotho said when they were inside. 'I thought we agreed you would come to me. I know people in Head Office. We could have come to an arrangement. You know Guka does not understand young people.'

'Thank you, sir. But don't worry. It is taken care of.'

'You now have some time. Think carefully about your life.'

'That is exactly what I am doing, sir.'

Ocuotho sighed, and looked at him. 'I have a small matter. A personal matter. My daughter is sick and I was wondering whether you could lend me something small. Maybe 10,000 shillings?'

'No problem. The usual interest applies. And I need a blank cheque.'

'Of course.' Ocuotho wrote a cheque and handed it over.

Kandle reached into his back pocket and counted out twenty 500-shilling notes from the furniture-loan money.

'Well, I suspect we won't be seeing you around here, one way or the other,' Ocuotho said, with some meaning. 'We'll miss...'

They both laughed from deep within their bellies, that laughter of Kenyan men that comes from a special knowledge. The laughter was a language in itself, used to climb from a national quiet desperation.

Billy Kahora is the managing editor of the Kenyan literary journal *Kwani?* and the author of the non-fiction book *The True Story of David Munyakei*. His writing has appeared in *Granta*, *Kwani?* and *Vanity Fair*.

Love on Trial

Stanley Kenani

MR LAPANI KACHINGWE'S POPULARITY HAS SOARED. He has always been popular because of his love for strong drink. But from the time he stumbled upon two young men in a toilet, his fame has reached levels he never imagined.

In principle his story is for free, whether he is sober or drunk, but in practice if you want to get down to the finest details, 'the juiciest parts' as he calls them, you have to buy him a tot of *kachasu*, the spirit distilled at Mr Nashoni's Village Entertainment Centre on the outskirts of Chipiri village.

In truth, nobody ever finds out what the strands of those details are in Mr Kachingwe's story. After listening to it many times, one comes to the conclusion that whatever happened in that toilet, the long and the short of it is that Mr Kachingwe caught two boys, one of whom is Chipiri village's own Charles Chikwanje and the other a stranger presumably from a neighbouring village, *in flagrante*.

'How is that possible,' is what most of the villagers want to know, 'between two men?'

'Another tot,' Mr Kachingwe answers. Or, when the inquisitive person looks better off financially, Mr Kachingwe may say: 'Give each one of us a tot, then you will have all the details,' to nods of approval from his drinking mates sitting under the huge *kachere* tree outside Mr Nashoni's house. The enquirer obliges. He throws what is called 'a round' – in the lingo used at places like Mr Nashoni's Village Entertainment Centre.

'OK, tots bought,' the round-thrower says, sitting down opposite Mr Kachingwe on a brown, short-legged stool. 'Now, tell me. Who, in the process, was performing the functions of the man and who was the woman, if I may be a little straightforward?'

Mr Kachingwe prefers to begin from the beginning. He does not remember what he must have eaten, he says, but he was coming from Mr Nashoni's, naturally not very sober, when his stomach was terribly upset beyond what he could bear. He saw a line of toilets outside the Chipiri Primary School, those brick iron-sheet-roofed pit latrines, about ten or so of them, right at the beginning of the school compound if you were coming from the western side. It was a Saturday, so there were no pupils at school. He ran for the toilets, burst into the first he came to and had relieved his stomach of its burden in one monumental effort when he realized he had company. Charles and a boy Mr Kachingwe failed to recognize were so engrossed in their act it took some time for them to become aware somebody had entered the toilet, by which time Mr Kachingwe had seen 'everything'.

'What,' the round-thrower asks, 'was the everything? I have heard the rest of the story many times over, but I want to hear the everything in greater detail.'

'Another tot,' Mr Kachingwe demands.

His patience beginning to wear out, the round-thrower obliges, faced with no choice. But when the contents of that second tot are poured down the throat at one go, Mr Kachingwe's speech begins to slur. A strong odour of alcohol escapes his mouth as he speaks. His eyes are redder than they were not so long ago. He tries to delve into the details but the story is not coherent at all. In despair, the round-thrower leaves, feeling cheated. Mr Kachingwe's drinking buddies laugh.

'Keep it that way, man,' the buddies say. 'Like that, we

won't worry about money to spend on alcohol until the end of September.' This, by the way, is the first week of August. Everybody laughs again. Another day at Mr Nashoni's Village Entertainment Centre is going on very well.

Every day the story spreads like oil poured on a sheet of white paper. Scores of people come to Chipiri to hear for themselves. They come from such distant villages as Ngulukira and Kayesa, even Mkanda in the neighbouring Mchinji district.

Maxwell Kabaifa, a short, bespectacled, balding, retired civil servant and Mr Kachingwe's former drinking buddy, now a born-again Christian, once tried to persuade Mr Kachingwe to desist from ruining the boy's future. 'He's one of only three of us from this village to have made it to the university,' he said. 'Don't you realize the state might send him to rot in jail?' Mr Kachingwe, towering over his childhood friend, said he learnt Civics in Standard Six in the local primary school and, among the qualities of a good citizen of any state on earth, telling the truth was of great importance. He was reporting the truth as he saw it. The consequences of the truth were none of his business.

As Maxwell Kabaifa feared, the story quickly attracted the attention of the police. Charles was arrested under Section 153 and 156 of the penal code for 'unnatural offences' and 'indecent practices between males'.

Charles was a student of law at the University of Malawi's Chancellor College. He was arrested in the summer holiday, after which he was due to enter his third year. He used his knowledge of the law to successfully fight for bail, which the police had initially resisted 'for the culprit's own safety'. Charles also used his knowledge of the law to totally refuse disclosing the name of his lover, in spite of being coerced by the police.

Now the village of Chipiri has become famous. Reporters from the *Malawi News* have been here. The day before, it was the *Weekend Nation*. Zodiak Radio Station was here, as was Capital FM, MIJ Radio, Star FM, Power 101FM, Joy Radio and MBC Radio 1. They all want to talk to Charles, to take his picture, and to ask him a lot of probing questions. Charles has refused to co-operate. When they come to his parents' house, right in the heart of the village next to the clump of banana trees, Charles refuses to meet them, so they end up talking to his father. His mother completely avoids the reporters. The father simply says he is quite shocked, like everybody else, but he loves his son and wishes him only the very best. 'I stand in solidarity with Charles,' he says. When the reporters ask more inconvenient questions, like 'Did you notice any homosexual traits in him before this scandal?' he answers: 'I have told you I stand by my son and that is enough for now.'

Naturally, being what is termed in the news world as a 'source', Mr Kachingwe has received major attention. Not long ago he was on the centre spread of both leading newspapers, tot in hand, with the tiny grass-thatched huts of Chipiri in the background.

Sales at Nashoni's have gone up many times, as the number of Mr Kachingwe's buddies increases exponentially. With these people from the city coming in to interview Mr Kachingwe, who still insists on the interview fee of a round being thrown, being Mr Kachingwe's friend has become a lucrative undertaking. Mr Kachingwe is also benefiting in other ways. Since some interviewers are so generous that they give him cash, he is not as skinny as he was before the scandal broke. He can now afford some meat and eggs and looks well fed.

The news has been picked up by the international media. The Associated Press was here, as was Reuters. The well-known Mr David Iphani, BBC correspondent and probably Malawi's best journalist of the moment, was the only one to persuade Charles to accept being interviewed. When the village heard it on the shortwave radio on *Focus on Africa* in the evening – for those few who could understand English – there was shock that Charles sounded unrepentant, even proud of what he called 'having come out in the open'.

'This,' Charles explained in his deep voice, 'is my natural orientation. I have never felt sexually attracted to any woman in my life.' David Iphani asked him: 'What about the law? Aren't you afraid of breaking the law?' Charles responded: 'If a law is designed to suppress freedom, then it is a stupid law that must be scrapped.'

Charles's response has attracted even greater national attention. Now reverends, pastors, prophets and apostles, even bishops, are saying on MBC and other radio stations that the young man needs to be prayed for. 'He needs deliverance,' says Apostle Dr Njole Kaluzi of the Last Church of Christ the Redeemer. 'Malawi is a God-fearing nation. We cannot allow satanic acts to taint our nation. Satan is using Charles, and we need to banish the devil from the young man's heart. Charles needs to accept Christ as his saviour. He needs to be born again.'

Exciting news: *Reach Out and Touch* is planning a talkshow-style live broadcast interview with Charles! *Reach Out and Touch* is a programme on MBC television which reaches out to, and touches the hearts of millions of viewers. Ordinarily the programme is designed to bring rare human-interest stories to the nation's attention, so that those who are touched to the heart might also be touched to the pocket to help the victim.

Through *Reach Out and Touch*, intelligent orphans failing to progress with their education due to lack of money for tuition have been assisted; as was Tinyade, a little girl who had a severe heart problem which could only be treated in an expensive South African hospital. The examples are endless.

At first Charles refuses to talk to the guys from MBC. He does not want this circus to continue. He has spoken to the media, has made his case, and that is enough for now. 'I am not like an animal in a zoo, to be viewed by the nation at large,' he tells his father by the fireside one evening, just after a dinner of very tasty local chicken with *nsima*.

But his father, a primary school teacher by profession, encourages him to accept the *Reach Out and Touch* challenge. 'The more you talk about it, the faster the public gets used to you and, as a result, might begin to accept you,' the older man says. So, in the end, Charles agrees to sit for this interview.

On the appointed day, three vehicles come from MBC. There is a green van on which is written 'Outside Broadcasting Unit'. There is a black Land Rover with more television equipment. The third vehicle, a red dual-cab Toyota Land Cruiser, carries the crew of cameramen, technicians and Khama Mitengo, the famous presenter.

Everybody in the village is curious. Children, dressed in all manner of torn shorts and short-sleeved shirts and almost all of them on bare feet, leave the playground to surround the cars. Men and women peep from their huts, others come out altogether, to take a good look at the crew from Malawi's only television station.

Mr Kachingwe is the first to come forward for the interview. The show takes place in one of the classrooms of the Chipiri Primary School. The crowd of spectators from the village sits behind the desks. A platform has been prepared at the front of the classroom where Khama sits facing the interviewee. The blackboard has been covered with a big, white sheet that proclaims: 'Reach Out & Touch'. The crew from MBC is scattered all over the room. Some stand in corners. Others have planted themselves inside the crowd to control it. The crowd are excited. Everybody's eyes are on Mr Kachingwe.

'Tell me,' says Khama, 'how did it all begin?'

Mr Kachingwe explains as he always has. He walks to the toilet with the TV crew and the crowd in tow. He shows them inside, pointing at the spot where the two men were when he stumbled upon them. After that, the show returns to the classroom, where Khama continues to ask for more details. When sober, Mr Kachingwe is a shy man, so he fails to explain more, repeats himself over and over, and trembles intensely due to *delirium tremens*, the DTs. It is visible on his face what a relief it is when Khama releases him.

Charles is called into the hot seat. '*Wamathanyula!* Homosexual!' the crowd roars. 'Let him show us how they do it!' Charles is steady. At about 1.75 metres tall, slim, with a long face, Charles is wearing jeans and a black T-shirt. On the T-shirt, written in white letters, is: 'Peace, love and unity'. He is wearing white sports shoes, and carrying what looks like the Holy Bible in his hands. He lowers his frame into the chair. One of the people from MBC, away from the camera's gaze, raises his hand to pacify the crowd. They become silent.

'So you are Mr Charles Chikwanje, the man in the news?' Khama begins.

'Yes, I am Charles Chikwanje.'

'Welcome to *Reach Out and Touch*, Charles.'

'Thank you.'

'You are a homosexual, as widely reported?'

'I am gay, yes.'

'What does it mean, exactly?'

'It means I am, by nature, somebody who is sexually attracted to another man.'

'Madman!' the crowd jeers. 'Evil man!'

'What is the name of your boyfriend?'

'I can't tell you.'

'Why?'

'I don't want him to be arrested.'

'Isn't that an obstruction of justice?'

'No, it is a show of love.'

'For whom? For the nation? For yourself? Or for homosexuality?'

'For my lover.'

The crowd laughs. 'Lover, my foot!' somebody says, and

the crowd laughs some more. The MBC man raises his hand to make them quieten down.

'Is it really true that a man can be born a homosexual? Or have you come into contact with Western ideologies? Were you introduced to the homosexual world by tourists, for instance?'

'That's incorrect. I have never interacted with anybody from the West. I have never read gay literature. Homosexuality is not Western and it's not an ideology. It is nature. One is born either heterosexual or homosexual. It's just the way I am. I was born like this.'

'Liar! Liar!' the crowd roars.

'Now Charles, tell me, how do you do it, man to man?'

'What?'

'The sex, how do you do it, man to man?'

'Are you married, sir?'

'No, why do you ask?'

'But surely, at your age you've had sex, no?'

'I don't see the relevance of this–'

'When you find a chance to have sex, how do you do it?'

Khama sits bolt upright, as if stung by a wasp on his lower backside. The crowd laughs. 'Are you mad?' Khama asks, his face visibly angry. 'How can you ask me such a stupid and obscene question live on air?'

'How, then, can you ask me such a private question on a live show like this?'

Khama subtly gestures at his manager. Looking into the camera, he says, 'Dear viewers, we're now going for a commercial break.'

The crowd goes wild. Some are laughing and others are beating desks and cheering, while many are jeering. 'Don't ask me such obscene questions, do you understand?' Khama says to Charles, shouting above the noise. 'Malawi is a God-fearing nation. We can't afford to offend our viewers with gross content.'

'If you confine yourself within the boundaries of decency,'

Charles responds, 'I will not ask such questions again. But beware, because stupid questions will only get stupid answers from me.'

The MBC man asks the people to stop making a noise. Silence and sanity prevail again. The show resumes.

'I understand you're a student?' Khama asks.

'Yes. But let me ask you a question.'

'Proceed.'

'Why have you come to interview me?'

'Your story is so unusual that we believe our viewers might find it intriguing.'

'Are you sure my story is very unusual?'

'Of course. I have never heard of any man who sleeps with other men. Not in Malawi.'

'Last year, in the *Daily Times*, there was the story of a man from Dowa district who slept with a goat; do you remember?'

'Yes, I remember reading that.'

'You will also recall that in court he said, in defence, that he slept with the goat because it had looked at him suggestively, no?'

Khama laughs and the spectators join in. 'Of course I remember that.'

'And he further reasoned that he had used a condom, no?' The crowd, once again, bursts into laughter. The crew member from MBC raises his forefinger to his mouth to stop the noise.

'Let's not overstretch it. I remember. But what is your point?'

'Why didn't you interview that man? Wasn't his story far more unusual than mine? I am in love with a human being, for God's sake. The human being loves me back. There is a two-way flow of emotions. Are you sure my story is stranger than that man's?'

'He was mad like you, Charles!' somebody in the crowd screams. Others clap hands and some cheer.

'Let's separate issues here,' says Khama. 'By interviewing you, *Reach Out and Touch* is not saying the man who committed the bestiality offence was right to do so. That was, indeed, extremely unusual. But, Charles, you must also appreciate the fact that it is unnatural for a man to sleep with another man.'

'Who says it is unnatural?'

'The Holy Bible says so. Romans, chapter one, verse 27 says: "And likewise also the men, leaving the natural use of the woman, burned in their lust one toward another; men with men working that which is unseemly, and receiving in themselves that recompense of their error which was meet." This was in reference to Sodom and Gomorrah.'

'But the verse you have just quoted does not clarify whether these men were punished for abandoning their wives or for having sex with each other. I like to think it was because of the former, which indeed was wrong, because extramarital sex is unacceptable anywhere in the world. But I want you to specifically quote me any verse that says being gay is sinful, or, to use your preferred terminology, that homosexuals will not enter the kingdom of heaven. Only then will I believe you.'

'Listen, I didn't prepare for this interview the way one prepares for a sermon.'

'Look, the Holy Bible talks about the love between David and Jonathan as being special,' Charles says, quickly flipping open the book in his hands. 'In the second book of Samuel, chapter one, verse 26, David says: "I grieve for you, Jonathan my brother; you were very dear to me. Your love for me was wonderful, more wonderful than that of women." Before this, we are told David and Jonathan kissed and exchanged the clothes they were wearing as gifts. Don't you read more into that relationship than a simple friendship between two men?'

'No, I don't. This was a mere platonic friendship, or *amor platonicus*, since you use a lot of Latin in law. In Plato's *Symposium*, one learns that with genuine platonic love, the beautiful or lovely other person inspires the mind and the soul and directs one's attention to spiritual things. Such was the nature of the friendship between David and Jonathan, that in their appreciation of each other, God's name was praised. Not the sick theory you're trying to conjure up here.'

'The last time I checked, Plato was not an authority on Christianity but on philosophy. Plato attributed what you've just said to Diotima, a prophetess of Zeus. How can you link a pagan god with Christianity? But back to David, tell me, why do you think David specifically chose to compare his love for Jonathan with a woman's? Do you yourself have a male friend whose love for you is more than a woman's?'

'We're talking about David here, the patriarch of Jesus Christ, the man who had 16 wives!'

'But he could have been bisexual, no?'

'Anyway, the devil, as Shakespeare says, sometimes quotes scripture for his purpose.'

'Are you suggesting I am the devil incarnate?'

'Well, look, Malawi is a God-fearing nation. The reason the law forbids this is because it is a sin. Full stop. We may argue whichever way we want, but this does not alter the truth.'

'Let's examine the mantra "Malawi is a God-fearing nation". How much evil takes place at night? What happens behind the closed doors of offices? What about in churches? Don't we hear of sexual affairs between priests and their flock?'

'Do you want to tell us that Malawi is not God-fearing? Should Malawi stop regarding herself as God-fearing just because a homosexual says so?' He is irritated.

'We're a secular state, by the way, not a theocracy. Only an individual can be regarded as God-fearing, but the collection of 14 million individuals that make up Malawi cannot be termed God-fearing. Among the 14 million there are rapists and murderers, corrupt government officials, thieves and those who sleep with goats.'

Looking very confused, Khama again nods at his manager and says: 'Let's go for a commercial break!' The crowd is getting angry and confused. Some are praising Charles, while others complain that the discussion is for the educated. They can't follow the complicated arguments.

The interview resumes amid handclapping and cheering and whistling which seems to be more in favour of Charles. In the third and final section, Charles loosens up a little bit and explains that he came to spend the summer holiday in the village because he wanted to see his lover. He had been offered a temporary attachment to NBS Bank's legal department where he might have earned a little money for himself during the holiday, but he had declined that opportunity because he missed his lover so much. Charles says he is happy his family understands him. No, he does not need any special prayers, thanks. He is deeply religious himself, a follower of Jesus Christ. No, he did not become gay because he is unlucky with women – on the contrary, he has ignored many women's advances at Chancellor College simply because he is not interested and cannot double-cross his lover. Charles further reveals that there is a lady – a daughter of a high-profile person – who has written him five letters of love, but he has politely declined entering into any relationship with a woman. In spite of Khama's insistence, Charles refuses to divulge any further details.

By the time he walks out, Charles has reclaimed much of his lost respect. Many people are talking about how eloquent he is. Others, of course, think he is blasphemous to suggest that there can be characters associated with gay behaviour in the Holy Bible.

The 'daughter of a high-profile person' Charles refers to is Nyenyezi who, as her name suggests, is as beautiful as a star. She is the youngest daughter of the President of the Republic of Malawi. She is Charles's classmate at law school. They became friends in the first year of their studies.

It started in the Law 120 class. When the lecturer taught

them Judicial Precedents, Nyenyezi struggled to understand the difference between *obiter dicta* and *ratio decidendi*. 'Oh, there is too much Latin in this subject,' Nyenyezi lamented, looking utterly lost. She enlisted the help of Charles, who appeared to be the brightest in class, for a better explanation.

'*Obiter dicta* are comments a judge says as a by-the-way sort of thing,' Charles explained, 'while *ratio decidendi* is the rationale for the decision. Don't let the Latin distract you at this stage because, from what I hear, we haven't seen anything yet.'

From then on, Charles became Nyenyezi's walking encyclopaedia. When they came to Theories and Practice of Constitutional Interpretation and Application in the Law 120 class, Nyenyezi consulted Charles to understand the difference between originalism – the original intent of the framers of the constitution – and non-originalism, new interpretations foreign to the intent of the original authors. As she admired the way that Charles explained these topics with ease, her admiration deepened to love. *Here is a handsome and intelligent man*, she thought.

Wouldn't our children have the blessing of being both beautiful and intelligent?

She began to shower him with gifts, frequently rare items from her father's Sanjika Palace. On his birthday she bought him a very expensive card shaped like a heart, which she sprinkled with sweet-smelling perfume. On Valentine's Day she gave him a red rose. When he seemed to show no interest at all, she began writing him letters, telling him she would do anything in this world to win a place of honour in the secret chambers of his heart. Charles ignored all this.

Now Nyenyezi, along with the whole country, has heard about the latest developments. She has written Charles a letter, telling him that she does not believe he was born gay. 'If you can let your heart taste the love of a woman,' she argues, 'you will realise that this gay orientation thing is a mere illusion, rectifiable by unlocking the gates of resistance for you to walk into the wonders of heterosexual love. I believe it's the inquisitiveness of youth that makes you enter into a relationship with another man.' She discreetly suggests that if they could publicly announce they are in love, his court case would freeze, given the immense powers of Nyenyezi's father.

Charles writes back. He argues that he feels insulted by suggestions that his being gay is a psychological problem. 'The truth is I have never been sexually attracted to any woman in my life and I do not think I ever will be. I am like this by nature. Sorry, I cannot betray my loved one by doing something against my conscience.'

Three days after the *Reach Out and Touch* interview, Charles appears before the magistrate of Kasungu town. He goes through a speedy trial. The Centre for Human Rights and Re-habilitation, a non-governmental organization, has provided him with a lawyer free of charge.

The state has one witness, a sober version of Mr Kachingwe. Charles has no witness.

Judgment is delivered on the fifth day after the commence-ment of the trial. Charles is sentenced to 12 years of imprisonment with hard labour, without an option of a fine. In passing this sentence, the magistrate has taken into account the key mitigating factor that Charles is a first-time offender, which is why the sentence is lenient. The convict is free to appeal against the ruling in seven days. The court rises. Charles is handcuffed and taken through a celebrating crowd outside to a Black Maria, while his mother collapses. His father, silently kneeling next to his wife to comfort her, refuses to talk to any reporters. Before being pushed into the van, Charles turns to the horde of television cameramen and journalists and flashes a V sign for Victory. His face is grim.

Britain is angry. America is annoyed. Norway is furious. France is outraged. Germany is livid. Through envoys, they have made their disappointment known to the Malawi government.

The official government spokesperson, the Honourable Mrs Josephine Liyati, who is also the Minister of Information, was on *News at Eight*, saying, 'Donors are threatening to cut aid but we don't care. We are a God-fearing nation. The wishes of Malawians should be respected. We will not be held to ransom by aid. We view this donor reaction as an affront to the dignity of our nation. Malawi is a sovereign state. Let them keep their aid, and we will keep our religious and cultural values.'

The donors, of course, cut aid.

Every week, news is coming that more countries are putting pressure on the government. Sweden has protested and so has Denmark. Ireland and Iceland are planning to raise the issue at the Universal Periodic Review, a human rights assessment that takes place every four years.

The results of aid being cut are beginning to show. There is no medicine in hospitals. Fuel has become so scarce that the government has begun 'fuel broadcasts', in which it is announced, without any hint of shame: 'The nation has fuel that will last us for one and a half days.'

Teachers are protesting because their salaries have been delayed for four months. Inflation is rising. Even Mr Kachingwe is complaining because a tot, at five kwacha before, is now four times as much, and Mr Nashoni does not accept drinking on credit.

There is no longer anybody ready to buy Mr Kachingwe a tot to hear more about Charles's story. It seems Mr Kachingwe has nothing more to say, besides repeating himself over and over, and sometimes creating new details nobody really believes can be true. Mr Kachingwe's number of friends has diminished drastically.

In prison, when the warders are not paid for three months,

they vent their anger on Charles. They beat him up. They deny him food. They lock him in solitary confinement. 'All this is because of you,' they say.

The government says it will not be in a position to distribute the subsidized fertilizer to poor subsistence farmers. Fertilizer will be sold at its open market value, which is 5,000 kwacha per bag. Farmers are furious. In private, they utter many words against the president and the cabinet ministers – words that do not reflect the status of Malawi as a God-fearing nation.

Just before the final trial of Charles Chikwanje, Mr Kachingwe and several other villagers underwent a voluntary HIV test, in response to a nationwide HIV campaign organized by the National AIDS Commission. The NAC set up tents on the football grounds of Chipiri Primary School, where villagers were received in confidence, counselled and tested. Mr Kachingwe tested positive for the virus. His CD4 count was found to be very low. The people from the NAC gave him some antiretroviral drugs as a start-up package. 'You must take one tablet a day,' a tall NAC official in a white coat and a black cap said. 'Never miss a single day. And you must stop taking alcohol.' Mr Kachingwe was advised to register himself at the nearby Health Centre to receive the ARV drugs every month.

A couple of months after the trial of Charles Chikwanje, Mr Kachingwe's ARV start-up package has ended. He goes to the Kamboni Health Centre to replenish the supply. 'Sorry,' says the clinical officer, 'ARVs have run out of stock throughout the country. We are told it's because the country that was donating them to Malawi has cut the supply.'

Mr Kachingwe returns home looking very sad.

Three months later, Mr Kachingwe begins coughing terribly. He spits up blood. Maxwell Kabaifa is the only friend from the old days who comes once in a while to cheer him up, but Kabaifa's ultimate objective is to convert Mr Kachingwe to Christianity of the Pentecostal variety.

Today, Maxwell Kabaifa picks a story from the pastor's sermon last Sunday. The two men are sitting on a bamboo mat under the mango tree behind Mr Kachingwe's house. Mr Kachingwe, now very skinny, is propped up by the trunk of the tree, his legs stretched out in front of him.

'A long time ago,' Maxwell Kabaifa begins, 'a farmer decided to trap an evasive rat. He set up a deadly mousetrap. When the rat saw the trap through a crack in the wall, he asked the cock to persuade the farmer to undo it, "because,' the rat argued, 'this is bad for us all". The cock, walking away, laughed and said, "That's not my business. It's a mousetrap, not a cocktrap." The rat, unhappy, went and asked a cow if she could help, only to receive a similar answer.

'Are you listening?'

'Yes, I'm listening, Maxwell, go on.'

'One night, the farmer's wife heard the trap snap. She rushed to investigate. However, something in the darkness bit her. The pain was so sharp, she yelped. The farmer rushed to her side with a paraffin lamp, only to see that there was a big, black snake trapped in there.'

'*Eish*, that's scary,' says Mr Kachingwe. 'I hate snakes.'

'So do I,' says Maxwell. 'Now, to proceed: as the health of the farmer's wife deteriorated, she lost her appetite. It became necessary to kill the cock in order to make chicken soup hoping to revive her appetite. The wife eventually died and the farmer decided to slaughter the cow to feed the gathering mourners. The rat watched all this with great sadness. He peeped through the crack in the wall and saw the farmer sitting dejectedly, badly in need of comforting. One day, deeply depressed by the loss of the wife he so loved, and continuously blaming himself for it, the farmer took a rope and hanged himself.'

Mr Kachingwe stares at Maxwell. His lips move as if to

say something, but the words do not come out. He trembles violently because of the *delirium tremens* and, after a full minute or two of silence, he nods: 'Nice story. A very nice story.'

Born in 1976, **Stanley Onjezani Kenani** is a writer from Malawi. *Love on Trial* is one of the short stories in his debut collection, *For Honour and other stories*, published in 2011 by Random House Struik in South Africa. In 2007, he was second runner-up in the HSBC-SA PEN award, judged by JM Coetzee, for the title story of his collection, which was also shortlisted for the Caine Prize in 2008. A poet who is also an accountant, Kenani lives and works in Geneva, Switzerland. He is currently finalizing his debut novel, *Drama Republic*.

La Salle de Départ

Melissa Tandiwe Myambo

LIKE SO MANY OMENS, she had missed its significance at the time. Three years ago, Ibou had sent home a photo of his fancy business-school friends in America. The thickish envelope had arrived after a long silence and Fatima had not felt the slightest presentiment as she pierced the envelope with a kitchen knife and withdrew the typed pages. She went outside to read the precious letter to Father.

The old man was ensconced under the mango tree, sitting on a short stool, leaning against the trunk's rough bark. His habitual grey *boubou* with swirly, yellow embroidery up the front was unravelling at the collar but billowed out grandly at his sides. Because he had been educated in Koranic School, he found it easier to read Arabic than French but these days he couldn't read much of anything because his vision was dimming with the advancing years. From a distance his eyes almost appeared blue, the dark irises encircled by rings of grey and the cornea covered by a film of translucent gel. Of late, those rheumy, shimmery eyes could only make out general shapes and so it was usually up to Babacar or another nearby grandchild to read him the tiny print of the daily newspapers.

Fatima waved the letter in front of him but he made a motion for her to wait, indicating the young men by the water tap preparing *ataya*. When it was ready, Lamine, their neighbour, offered the old man the first taste of the second round. The sun shone through the small glass cup. The piping hot tea was almost darker than the old man's trembling hand. He took a sip and sucked his tongue as the zing of the syrupy sweet brew hit it with full force. He nodded his head in approval as he handed the glass to Fatima. She took a sip and then handed it back to Lamine, who walked back to the other young men huddled around the primus stove and the little kettle. They were already heaping more tealeaves into the simmering water and dropping in more sugar cubes for the third round.

Father nodded at her to begin reading the letter and it was only then that she noticed the photograph that had slipped out from between the pages. Picking it up, she gently shook the dust off of it and wiped it on her *pagne*. It was Ibou with two other young men and two girls standing on the steps of what looked like a library or some other majestic university building propped up by ornately decorated columns. To Fatima, it looked like a concrete wedding cake. She had barely taken note of Ghada, assuming that perhaps the Nigerian girl with chiselled features was Ibou's *petite copine*, even though the letter contained a whole paragraph dedicated to this wonderful Ghada: 'She's Egyptian and she plays women's soccer. Plus, she speaks fluent French and English and she has read the entire Koran in Arabic! She is head of MESO – Middle Eastern Students' Organization. That's how we met because I am head of ASA – the African Students' Association. We organized a conference on Arab-African trade together. Many important dignitaries came, thanks to Ghada's organizational skills, and Ghada...'

The old man held up his hand and she paused. He called Lamine over and gave him some crumpled bills to go and buy more sugar for the third round of *ataya* still boiling. The letter made him happy, he proudly told every passer-by that Ibou was keeping up with the faith even though he was all the way over *theeerrrre* in America. Fatima re-examined the photo: all she saw was an unfortunately petite girl who looked like the daughter of one of the Lebanese merchants in town.

Now, looking back, it was incredible that she had not felt

any special premonition about this woman. Instead, she had shown the photo to Maimouna, her best friend, who agreed that Ghada looked Lebanese. 'Christian or Muslim, they all switch men daily like their fancy French brassieres.' Fatima had nodded knowingly, not that she associated with those Lebanese women herself, besides buying in their shops or restaurants, but this is what Maimouna said and Maimouna would know. 'She's very short,' clucked Maimouna disapprovingly.

✳ ✳ ✳

The car gurgled into life at Uncle Djiby's fourth try. Hearing the scratchy sound, Fatima withdrew her hands from the basin of tepid water in which she was planning to soak the *bouye* overnight. It lay next to the bowl, desiccated fruit of the baobab, still crumbly dry and white. She glanced around for Ibou, about to open her mouth and call to him in her high-pitched voice. There he was, imprisoned in the puddle of light cast by the solitary street lamp, hunkered down close to the ground, his chin thrust forward and his chest pressed against his thighs. She knew he was trying to suppress his irritation by drawing stick figures in the sandy soil. It was something he used to do when he was still a skinny, knock-kneed boy. The familiarity of the action plucked her back across a desert of forgotten memories. A long-buried affection swelled in Fatima's breast. There *was* a time when they had been close. Perhaps he still remembered fondly the long-gone days before he went to live in America, when he used to mimic her high voice, 'e-e-e-e-e-e-e-e-e', saying it reminded him of a mosquito's whine. Would he agree to help her now – during this rushed two-week holiday in Senegal after so many years away in America – in honour of that former time?

Uncle Djiby revved the engine and beamed genially, unashamed of his car, which was almost older than Ibou. Once upon a time, it had been a brand new Renault but now it was a box of battered tin on wheels, painted yellow and black to show it was a taxi. Fatima and Ibou both climbed into the back seat since Ibou's hand luggage and laptop were filling up the front one. She could feel how tense his body was, rigid with annoyance; she forced herself to lean back into the lumpy seat and willed herself to relax so that he in turn would also.

He'd wanted to flag a taxi from the streets, something larger and more comfortable, like one of the newer Peugeots. She also suspected that he would have preferred to go to the airport alone but he hadn't dared to flat out suggest it, merely muttering something about how it would be much more time efficient. Fatima had pretended not to hear him because that's not how things were done, after all.

As the car lumbered off on its bald tyres, just barely skimming the patchwork tarmac, dipping precariously into multiple potholes, Uncle Djiby flipped through his extensive collection of pirated cassettes with one hand and then slipped in the latest Baaba Maal album. A static-creased mbalax-influenced reggae tune started up. Ibou leaned forward jerkily, raising a finger to tap Uncle Djiby on the shoulder, about to protest the poor sound quality, when his cellphone beeped. He flipped it open. A second later he cackled out loud and his face suddenly relaxed, his lips unpursing and his eyebrows moving apart. Fatima breathed a little easier. She had been examining his stony exterior for days, searching desperately for a breach in which to wedge her request. 'Will you share the joke?' she asked gently.

'It's a text message from Ghada. I can't believe my roaming is finally working again and, of course, just in time for me to go to the airport.'

Ghada, always Ghada! 'What does she say?'

'Too much testosterone, not enough balls.'

Fatima raised an eyebrow.

Ibou chuckled to himself, 'She must be *really* mad: too much testosterone, not enough balls! That's a good one.'

He was unconsciously speaking in English, quoting Ghada verbatim.

Fatima, uncomprehending, removed her chewing stick from her mouth and smiled politely. As she would smile at a stranger or a foreigner, even though Ibou was her brother – same mother, same father.

'It's difficult to translate,' he suddenly realized what he had done and guiltily resumed in Wolof. 'She is calling me…' he cast around for a word, '…a sheep.' He hesitated and then continued, 'She said I don't stand up to my family enough.'

Since Fatima didn't understand English, she was so grateful for his translation that she nodded to show that she got it now, but as the meaning of these words began to crystallize, her vigorous nodding abruptly ceased. Her emerald-green damask foulard slipped back and Ibou noticed for the first time that there were strands of silver streaking through her closely plaited hair. How old was she now? Almost 40 probably.

There was a short silence as Fatima's mind kneaded this chunk of information, trying to make it digestible. Her concentration was broken by Baaba Maal's soprano sinking into her consciousness. She tried to blot out the music. What position did Ghada, not even his *wife*, occupy for her to wield such power in the affairs of the family? Who was she to tell Ibou to 'stand up to his family' when the family was bonded by blood and name and she was nothing but an interloper? Would Ibou care more about this Ghada's opinion than the heartfelt request of his very own sister?

A sigh escaped her lips. Her mind was not nearly as nimble as her fingers. She could take a shallow brown basket full of rice, her long fingers whisking through it, searching for weevils and pebbles, separating them out, shaking the grains again, searching, separating, until the rice was ready to cook, all in the time it takes to scramble an egg. But her mind was slow, it moved like *lait caillé*, sweet, curdled milk, lumpy, glutinous, creamy.

'But is she your wife?' she ventured finally, twisting a gold filigree ring around her middle finger. It was longer than the first joint of her finger and the pointy tip grazed her bony knuckle.

'Not technically… but she will be soon. We live together.'

'Yes, I believe you mentioned that but I thought she was very religious.'

'She is.'

Again a nod. This time noncommittal. Fatima looked through the window as Uncle Djiby's ramshackle taxi ploughed through Dakar's dark, dusty streets.

'She *is* very religious,' Ibou repeated himself and she could hear the defensiveness salting his voice.

'No, no, I understand. *Of course.*' She hadn't meant to be denigrating but what god-fearing Muslim woman dared to take the veil while sharing the bed of a man not her husband? Not that Fatima was one to cast stones but, at this moment, this all-powerful Ghada stood between her and her son's future. Ghada was like a big black stone that could splinter your teeth if it wasn't removed before the rice was cooked.

'Ghada has read the whole Koran,' Ibou said aloud, echoing his long-ago letter. 'Religion for her is something she truly practises rather than obeys. It's something that she interrogates and interacts with, wrestling with its contradictions and inconsistencies, those within her and those within the religion itself. She is not afraid of them, you see, she doesn't deny them, she faces them head on. We can only understand God's word as it is translated by and through men. God is great but all religions are man-made and are therefore imperfect.'

Fatima held her breath. Were these Ibou's words or Ghada's? He sounded like he was reading from a book but his hands were empty. She had never known Ibou to be either religious or philosophical. Not trusting herself to reply, she slipped the foulard off and then expertly rewrapped the thick, starchy material around her head. She lowered her arms and twitched her shoulders so that the heavy gold embroidery bordering her collarbone shifted to the side leaving her left shoulder bare in the preferred style. It was her most expensive boubou, the one she had worn for Maimouna's fourth child's baptism. This entire readjustment took almost two whole minutes yet Ibou's gaze was still fixed on her expectantly. Was she actually supposed to respond to that speech? Her mind churned to no avail.

Finally relenting, Ibou looked away and pulled his red baseball cap further down on his brow and turned his iPod back on, jamming the headphones deep into his ears. He was wearing baggy jeans and a navy blue T-shirt with 'Brooklyn' scrawled across the front. On his feet were oversized sneakers. He looked like a character out of an American movie, especially with the pea-sized headphones plugged into his ears blasting a thumping, gritty bass that clashed with Uncle Djiby's music. Maybe this little white machine was whispering secret incantations to him, bribing him, convincing him, just like Ghada, that he shouldn't listen to her.

Fatima closed her eyes and leaned back into the car's filthy seat. The deep red seat cover was cracked and tufts of dusty, yellow foam spurted out in places like little mushrooms. Uncle Djiby's dilapidated taxi was the best vehicle she could rustle up under the circumstances. The whole family had gone to Kaolack for Adja's funeral but someone had to stay behind to accompany Ibou to the airport. Of course, the whole family was outraged that he hadn't changed his ticket and stayed at least an extra week. Adja was their father's eldest sister after all. No-one expected him to stay for the entire 40 days of mourning but at least a week.

'But you have to work every day in America,' Fatima said in his defence.

'And the last time you were in America was when exactly?' Maimouna was her closest friend from childhood but, to be honest, Maimouna's relationship with Ibou was not that different from her own. Perhaps it was the 12 years between their ages that rendered their relationship so constrained by formalities. Or was it all the years that Ibou had spent in America, years that stretched out like the great desert to the north? Or was it something she couldn't quite get hold of, like a fishbone buried deep in slippery flesh, avoiding extraction by the fingers yet fatal to the gullet?

Now time was running out and she still hadn't asked Ibou for the one thing that she wanted to happen above everything else. How to begin? Gathering her courage under her tongue, she opened her mouth to speak but just then, Uncle Djiby switched off the staticky tape. Keeping his fingers on the steering wheel, his large head swivelled all the way around, balancing precariously on his long, delicate neck. He flashed his chocolate-brown teeth, coloured by the waters of his Kaolack youth, 'So Americain Boy, can you get me a new cellphone? I hear they're cheaper over there.' He used the English word boy. He had started calling Ibou 'Americain Boy' on his first trip back to Senegal and Ibou hated the nickname. He almost flinched but muttered through gritted teeth, 'I'll get you a cellphone if you get me to the airport in one piece.' He pointedly jammed his iPod earphones back into his ears.

'I'll take that as a yes, then. You can send it to Fatima's address. How long until you get there?' Slowly, his head, heavy with thick, springy locks and seemingly too weighty for his neck, turned back to face the front. Ibou grudgingly turned off his iPod. 'I am flying Dakar to Paris and then Paris to New York. I'll be there tomorrow.'

'*Inschallah,*' Uncle Djiby intoned emphatically. Trans-Atlantic flights still seemed like an affront to God's will.

Ibou didn't repeat the phrase after him. He just kept staring steadily out the window. In the yellow light of the streetlamps, his profile didn't appear to soften. Where had that little boy gone to, Fatima wondered, the one who used to write them long letters every week, begging to come home?

Fatima tapped her ring against the car door, metal on metal. Her mind worked along the clicking rhythm, calculating and recalculating her finances. Since her divorce five years ago, her brain had transformed into a calculator, adding and subtracting continuously, even in her sleep. Babacar was fast outgrowing his clothes and she doubted he would have even one decent boubou to wear in Kaolack at the funeral. His father couldn't be relied on to give any more money since his new wife had just had twins. All her sisters had their own children to look after. They were an unlucky family since they were all daughters except for Ibou.

Perhaps she would have more choices if she had more brothers to rely on. Brothers were like the wind, they could go places she could not. She was like the sand. She could only be blown by the wind. But now she had a son and Ibou had to help her build wings for him. Her dream was for Babacar to go and live with his Uncle Ibou all the way, theeerrre in America, to go to school there, sow success for the family there and harvest green US dollars to bring back here.

'He's a good boy!' she blurted suddenly. Her hands raked the air as she tried to grab the words and stuff them back into her mouth. But too late.

'Of course he is. All mothers think their sons are good little boys.' He didn't seem jarred by her outburst, almost as if he had been expecting it.

How many times had she politely alluded to the idea of Babacar studying in America, hoping that Ibou would pick up her implications like so many threads and wind them into a spool of his own making. Then it would seem like it was his idea, the family would praise him, and she would be spared the humiliation of pleading outright. By means subtle and skilled, she had been leading him in this direction but he had refused to take the bait and finally, he had forced her hand. She drew a deep breath, 'Will you take Babacar to America next year to live with you?' There. It was out. The subject had been broached, not the way she had wanted it to be but there was no going back now.

Briefly, she closed her eyes, holding her breath, trying to return to the richness of that split second earlier this evening when the moist sweetness of the date splattered onto her tongue after a long, dry, dusty day of fasting. As a child, she had thought that eating candy would dulcify her words, make them come out sweet as young coconut milk. Now, she prayed that she could utter words palatable enough to open a path to America for young Babacar.

As she fasted all day, her mind stirred furiously, searching for the right words. For lunch, she cooked Ibou his favourite meal, making sure to add plenty of peanut paste to the *maffé* so that the sauce was reddish, thick and tasty. But even though he refused to actually fast, Ibou, in deference to Ramadan, had eaten less than usual. At *iftar*, just after sunset, there had been various interruptions from relatives and neighbours come to bid Ibou farewell and *bon voyage* again.

Again. He was always leaving. Her memories of him were distilled down to a series of departures, snapshots of ever leaving. And now he was leaving without having agreed to take Babacar with him. It was her turn to fix her gaze on him, willing him to respond in the affirmative...

When his reply finally came, it sailed out on a sigh, deep as the ocean that normally lay between them. 'But what would I do with an 11-year-old boy in New York? How would Ghada and I cope?'

Again this Ghada! Why was Ghada – not even his *wife* – hovering between them, like some unholy *djinn*, threatening her son's future?

Her mind marched forwards, falling into the icy sea between them, flailing around for facts that she could use in her favour. Hadn't Ibou himself left for the first time when he was only a few years older than Babacar, bandy-legged, scabby-kneed, the youngest of seven children but the only boy and hence, therefore, thus, so it was that he had grown wings under his feet while hers grew heavy, her toes gnarled like the roots of the baobab tree. But she wasn't as lucky as the baobab, she couldn't flourish in this semi-arid desert. No. She had grown thin; her collarbone poked above her boubou's neckline and her scrawny neck bulged with cords. But Ibou was stout, not just around the gut, like some wealthy, older men, but even around the knees, at the wrists. He was well-padded.

Before her divorce, she had been plumper but not as plump as she had been before she was married of course. '*Dafatooy*' was what they used to say about her, 'She's soft, fleshy, sexy.' She thought longingly of those plump, contented days but she quickly caught herself, refusing those self-pitying memories that could paralyse her the way the haunting melody of Mandingo *kora* music would make her stop dead in her tracks and echo in her ears the rest of the day. She shook herself, literally and figuratively, trying to think of how God had helped her. At least, she reminded herself, at least her business had grown, especially in the last two years.

✳ ✳ ✳

'What will you do?' asked Maimouna, soon after the divorce, and Fatima had looked at her blankly. Maimouna was washing clothes and her thick, strong arms were soapy up to her elbows. '*Mané*, what will you do for money? Can Ibou in America help you?'

Fatima mutely shook her head. 'I wouldn't want to ask him.'

'So what will you do then? Do. Do. For money,' Maimouna exclaimed, waving her hands around so that soap bubbles splattered all over the courtyard, trapping the sun in rainbow prisons wherever they landed on the hard-packed dirt until the wind pierced them and the bubbles burst. It was so pretty that Fatima almost cried, but then again, in those days, anything could make her cry.

The exception to her unhappiness was her first and only child: Babacar. Both families were grateful, hers and her husband's. Even though she never fell pregnant again, at least she had borne a boy and she never ceased to thank God for that, even while she prayed for more children. Seven years of barrenness rotted away her marriage until it was tart as the lemons fat girls sucked on to lose weight. Finally, they divorced. Not long afterward, her husband remarried. She had always refused to let him take a second wife, preferring divorce. But still she had her little man, a son, so much better than a daughter. A son could fly, a daughter could only nest. She had waited a long time for *le mariage* and for Babacar, and even though there was *le divorce*, she still had Babacar and she needed to invest everything she had in him. Everything. Except these days, she had nothing but tears. If only she could stop crying.

That very morning, she had quarrelled with a truculent adolescent and ended up sobbing. He was one of those poor boys who went into the bush to trap dozens of tiny, brown birds which he stuffed into an overcrowded cage and then brought to the city pavements where passers-by paid him a small fee to liberate one of the birds he had earlier captured. People said that as the bird flew away, it would bring happiness to the one who had purchased its freedom. But it was such a hot, dusty day and the birds were too many for the tiny cage. They were agitated, flitting in futility against the wooden bars. She just wanted them out, all of them, as if watching them fly away would prod something into bursting open deep inside of her.

She had tried to bargain with him in the usual manner but he was stubborn and she didn't have enough money to let them all go. She had offered him some of the thick and creamy *thiakry* she was carrying to her elder sister's home but still he refused.

'*Nercna trop*,' she said cajolingly but he looked at her balefully.

'Really,' she said in her sweetest voice, 'I am the best cook in all of H.L.M.'

Bending down, he picked up the cage, accidentally scraping his dusty calf. The birds twittered frenziedly. 'Please,' she implored him.

'Leave me alone!' he exclaimed sharply as he dived into the

street, dodging several taxis and a blue and yellow *car rapide* which had to brake suddenly, tilting unsteadily for a second. The *apprenti*, hanging on to the flapping back door, swore at the boy and the boy swore back. From the safety of the other side of the road, he threw her an accusing look that hit her with an almost physical force. It was the kind of look reserved for the mentally unbalanced. Hot tears were cascading down her cheeks, surprising her with their wetness. She hadn't known she was crying. Taking the cloth that lay across the platter of *thiakry*, she pressed it hard into her eye sockets, blotting the tears.

'I can cook.' The words popped out of her mouth.

Maimouna smiled and plunged her hands back into the soap suds. 'I'll say,' she said drily.

That's how it began, small, informal, on the street in front of her father's house. She had begun by selling sweet, fried *beignets* and cold *bissap* juice. Her fingers were always stained red from the hibiscus but she didn't care. At least she was earning something. With her marginal profit, she invested in buying some cups and spoons and she branched out into *lakh, thiakry* and *ngalakh* and soon she had a thriving clientele. Word of her delicious puddings spread to other areas and, in reply to queries about her 'secret ingredient', she would smile mysteriously.

But she still wasn't making much money until Maimouna's brother-in-law had put her in touch with Madame Diouf. Madame Diouf owned three restaurants that catered to well-to-do locals, expatriated Senegalese returned on holiday and high-budget tourists. Her menu promised the best of traditional Senegalese fare and her prices assured her clientele that they were receiving the very highest quality. Of course, Fatima only received about 10 per cent of what the customer paid but still, supplying three restaurants on a daily basis had turned her from a street-seller into an entrepreneur. She even had assistants now, two of them, plus a delivery boy on a moped who put the plastic buckets of *thiakry* and *ngalakh* into a cooler box, precariously strapped behind his seat. She could expand still further if only she could sell to other restaurants but Madame Diouf had forbidden this. Yet, she needed to expand to increase her revenue so that she could send Babacar to a better school. Children were like seeds that needed to be watered with lots of education. Then, like the mango tree, they would perennially bear fruit.

Or best of all, he could go to America. The fruit would be that much sweeter.

✷ ✷ ✷

'Do you not have the resources to look after Babacar, Brother?' Her high voice was deeper than usual as she tried to sound calmly persuasive, even though her tongue felt fuzzy with a film of unspoken words.

Ibou pulled the brim of his red cap further down on his forehead so that his eyebrows were almost covered. His lips were pursed again and he didn't look at her as he said tersely, 'It's not a question of resources.'

Fatima frowned in confusion. 'But do you have enough to support Babacar? Growing boys can be expensive – food, clothing, school fees. Do you have enough for all of that? I could try and send you some funds to help out.'

A harsh bark of laughter hushed her, shamed her. He flipped his cap back up his forehead. 'That wouldn't go very far. Do you have any idea how weak the CFA is compared to the US dollar?' He looked at her with flashing eyes. His mouth opened and closed. Of course she didn't know, why would she? It was just one more translation he was used to making and she was not.

'I'm sorry,' she said, her chin falling forward onto the scratchy gold embroidery. Her mind felt like it was boiling over. Was there any way she could make money in foreign currency?

'It's not a question of *money*. I have enough money for

God's sake. It's a question of...' he stumbled as he sought the translation. All he could think of was the English word 'lifestyle'. The flow of angry words filtered off as he finished with a feeble '...the way we live'.

Fatima shook her head in utter incomprehension. Ibou's hands landed palm down, fingers splayed, splat on to his jean-clad thighs: 'We have lives, we are busy people, we barely have time for each other.'

'Time?' she asked, her voice small. 'Babacar won't need any of your time.'

Now the heels of his palms dug deep into his eyes, reddening the whites. 'You don't understand. I work long hours, Ghada works long hours. We struggle to find...' his mind stumbled on 'quality time', but again he faltered and mistranslated as 'enough time to spend together. Our work schedules are so demanding plus the constant travel. Where is the time for an 11-year-old boy?'

Fatima's voice was pitched higher as she grew animated: 'But he knows how to cook, how to clean. He knows very well how to look after himself. In fact, he can be a help to you, keep the house for you when you are away!'

'We have a housekeeper, for God's sake. What I'm trying to say is that we have no *space* for him in our lives,' said Ibou in French.

'Aahhh,' Fatima's face came to life. 'Because you only have one bedroom?' Her voice was tinged with relieved laughter. 'But that is no problem. Babacar can sleep in the living room. That's where he sleeps now and he's always up early. He won't disturb you at all. I don't want you to spoil him.'

Uncle Djiby twiddled with the cassette player and Assane Mboup's latest hit came on. He also seemed relieved that the problem had been solved and laughed at them through the rearview mirror. 'Coolfinenice,' he said in English, his small, sleepy eyes crinkling in mirth under the thick locks straggling around his jovial face.

How much marijuana does the guy smoke? Ibou wondered

silently. He put his hand on the side of his leg and started to flex his quads, holding the muscle tense and then letting it relax. Besides the muffled music blaring from Djiby's cheap cassette player and the gentle sound of Fatima rhythmically gnawing on her chewing stick, there was quiet.

Outside the car window on the dimly lit streets, ghostly white mounds hunkered down by the roadside, the *moutons*. In a couple of months' time, when he would be far away, there would be sheep sold on every corner. The country would be preparing for Tabaski when every Muslim family would slaughter a sheep. Ibou could relate. Long ago, his family had sacrificed him to the call of America. But there was a trade-off buried in the fine print. Now he was supposed to sacrifice all he had gained for them. Up to and including every last penny and his relationship with Ghada, too, apparently. Uncle Djiby's cellphone, Aunt Marietou's new shoes for so-and-so's wedding, Little Aliou's new bicycle, Great Uncle Assane's new sewing machine, Adja's funeral expenses and now taking Babacar to America, the last in a long list of requests that were emptying him from the inside out. Hadn't he just texted Ghada yesterday: 'I feel like an ATM machine.'

He should have seen it coming. Why else had Fatima presented him with all the boy's report cards and bored him with long, detailed stories about his exploits on the soccer field? But this was well beyond the usual monetary request. This was asking him and Ghada to raise a young boy. Ibou had turned 28 last month. Ghada was two years older but how could he even ask her?

Fatima seemed lost in her own thoughts, a calm smile playing around her lips, Uncle Djiby's thick locks swung to the tempo of the music. They seemed to think the issue was settled.

'It's not because we have just one bedroom.' His voice was quiet, almost embarrassed.

Confusion crossed Fatima's face again, turning her eyes a dead coal black.

'There's just no room.'

'You don't have a living room? He can even sleep in the kitchen.'

Ibou clamped his teeth shut, accidentally biting his tongue. Blood oozed out, warm and gooey. 'I'm sure he is so perfect that we could just fold him up and put him away in the coat closet. Or can he sleep standing up?' The sarcasm was lost on her.

She took her chewing stick out of her mouth and pointed the masticated end at him, 'He's a good boy.'

Memory mocked him. Wasn't that what they used to say about him?

***

'He's a good boy.' Uncle Thierno, Djiby's eldest brother, had come home one dry August. He had brought his sister – Ibou's mother – a gold watch with little diamonds at the centre of the pale gold face. How they glittered in the sun, those diamonds. Just before doing the washing, she would take the watch off her wrist and lay it on a stone. The tightness of the band would still be etched on her skin as she dipped her dark hands into the soapy water. The raspy sound of wet cloth being rubbed together still reminded him of his mother, as did cheap watches sold by West African immigrants on 34th Street in New York. He smiled to himself, bemused by the appalling naiveté of that youthful Ibou. They had all been so impressed with Uncle Thierno's 'wealth'. 'He's a good boy,' the whole family kept repeating over and over, like the mantra of some kind of fanatical cult, until, at the end of August, Thierno agreed to take Ibou back with him. A forged birth certificate was produced, naming Ibou as Thierno's son. It was hard to get American visas! *C'est difficile dê!*

That September he started high school in a Maryland suburb even though he couldn't speak a word of English. His ESL classes were full of Korean and Dominican kids so he learnt Spanish faster than English and wrote letters home every week in a mixture of French and Wolof, full of stories of a life he found alienating and confusing. At night when he showered, he would pretend he wasn't crying as the water ran down his face. Instead, he would think about how lucky he was. *C'est difficile dê!* He would only do the early morning and last evening prayers, and he would pray to be allowed to go home, even for one day. His obsession with time travel spurred him on to learn English as he devoured science-fiction books. Madeleine L'Engle's *A Wrinkle in Time* became a talisman and he carried it everywhere with him.

When he finally graduated high school three years later, Uncle Thierno gave him a present. A ticket home. When he got there, he found his elderly mother had had a stroke. She was lying in a darkened room with long gauzy curtains catching the dusty sunshine. A newly married Fatima was looking after her, carefully sponging her arm so as not to get water on her watch, which had turned a burnished metallic colour. It no longer told the time. Two of the diamonds had fallen out of place and rolled around the pale gold face.

'Why didn't you tell me?' asked Ibou, aghast, holding his mother's other leathery palm. Her hand still felt strong, muscular.

'We didn't want to disturb your studies,' said Fatima, careful to avoid the swell of her pregnancy as she picked up her mother's leg and gently bent it. She ran the wet cloth up her shin bone. Ibou looked away, embarrassed somehow. It's not that he had never seen his mother's legs. Like all the little boys, he had spied on many a *sabar* and seen her dance to the *griot*'s drums, shedding her *pagnes* until the very last one, her legs exposed up to the fleshy inner thighs. Rather, he was embarrassed because she was inert, her leg muscles slack, like a floppy rag doll.

'When did this happen?' he asked quietly, his eyes averted.

'Six months ago.'

'Can she talk?'

'No,' Fatima shook her head. 'Not yet,' she quickly amended.

'Will she get better?'

'*Inschallah*.' She clasped her hands around the tight drum of her belly as if sucking in all of God's will for her own unborn child too. '*Inschallah*.'

At the end of Ibou's summer vacation, he flew back to the States against his will. His mother was near to death and he knew that if she died when he was overseas, he would never be able to make it back in time for the funeral. But they wouldn't let him stay. University was beginning in the Fall: it was everything they had all been working for. Hadn't Uncle Thierno offered to pay for Fatima's university expenses after she finished *lycée* with such high marks? But no, instead, her father said better to use that money for young Ibou, send him to a good Catholic school where he could learn proper French and improve their chances for future success.

'Fatima will wait to get married,' he informed the family. 'Ibou will go to school.'

***

'*Je vous en prie*,' she began in French and continued in Wolof, 'Please.' Her voice was hoarse. 'Only you can help him. Please help him to be like you. Do what Uncle Thierno did for you. Look how lucky you are, how successful. The success of one is the success of the whole family. Babacar's future is the future of us all.' She clutched at him, her long ring scratching his wrist as she grabbed his hands, pulling him around to face her.

He looked at her for a long time but he couldn't hold her gaze. It wasn't so much that he was afraid of what he would see but rather of what she would see, the feelings he did not care to admit even to himself. Somewhere deep down, Ibou experienced familial obligation as an intolerable irony. When his mother passed away in October of his first term at university, a strange aloofness was born in him. He never mourned her. It all happened so far away, in another time and place. Instead, all his childhood memories were slowly suffused with a sepia tint typical of old-fashioned photos, the type of photos one looks at but feels no connection to. Somewhere along the way, Senegal had died for him. It was all too abstract, too removed from his daily reality; family responsibility weighed on him but not as heavily as he felt it should. How many years had he been away? Half his life had been spent in another country, in another culture, where the ties of family do not strangle one's bank account and stifle one's emotional resources. He wished he felt more guilty. If he were a better person, he would.

'I can't take him with me. I just can't.'

'But why not?'

'How can I? I don't live like that.'

'Live like what?'

He dragged his hands away and leaned forward so that his forehead was against Uncle Djiby's seat. Uncle Djiby hummed to the music, far away in his own world. 'How do you know this is the best thing for him?' he spoke into the ripped upholstery.

'What could be better?'

'Don't you know that once he leaves home, he can never come back again?'

Fatima's hands were still resting near his jean-clad thigh. She pulled them back and began twisting the ring round and round her finger, scraping the filigree against her knuckle. Why was Ibou speaking in tongues? She was confused. 'I know the airfare is expensive but at least, hopefully, he will make it home once every few years.'

'It's not the airfare! Everything with you is money, money, money. I am not talking about money.' He turned his face and glared at her accusingly.

Fatima gasped at the waves of hot, choking anger emanating from him, like the winds of the *harmattan*.

Ibou closed his eyes in exasperation. He wished Ghada were here so that she could speak for him. She understood this unbearable duality of being. She would explain that when he came back to Dakar, he saw it through eyes made sensitive to dust, to hygiene, to other ways. When Fatima reached into the communal serving bowl to expertly shred the *cebujen's* vegetables with her nimble right hand, all he could think about was the dirt under her fingernails. And yet, she was being a good hostess, showing him typical Senegalese hospitality, the famed *teranga sénégalaise*. Her fingers worked fast and a lump of carrot landed in the groove from where he was shovelling his rice away. As fast as the rice disappeared, Fatima pushed more towards him, encouraging him to eat, eat, eat.

Delicious! An excellent cook, but why was the squat toilet never flushed properly? Why were there always lumps of other people's shit floating next to the footpads? He pushed the carrot around with his tongue, trying not to think about that and he wished he felt guiltier for constantly thinking about it. But he couldn't stop himself. Ghada was luckier in that sense, she was closer to her family. But then again, her family was different.

When Ghada spoke to her wealthy grandmother on the phone, she spoke in flawless French. He would tease her for hours afterwards, mocking her snobbish, clipped accent. Ghada's grandmother was part of that élite, Egyptian generation educated by the French. They were more at home in the wide boulevards of Paris than the narrow, winding alleys of Cairo's popular neighbourhoods.

It pushed him solidly in the chest, like Uncle Thierno's stubby forefinger when he wanted to make a point, something he had known for a long time but never wanted to formalize by putting it into actual words: Ghada was close to her family because this extremely inconvenient difference in income-earning potential didn't exist between them. Money bound people together just as much as it pushed them apart. Especially the intangible things money could buy, like lifestyles.

His mind turned over. He was running near the cliffs now but he couldn't turn away from where his mind was leading him.

Inconvenient. Poverty was very inconvenient. It led to extreme dependency, the opposite of self-sufficiency, which is exactly what Ibou had been trying to achieve for all these years. Couldn't the whole ethos of America be distilled into the essence of self... self-sufficiency, self-made, self-love... self, self, self... where did it cross over into selfishness?

He had almost died of homesickness the first three years in Maryland. Each turned out as cold as the other, the shiny snow and the language that sounded like coins being shaken in a tin. Both had appeared beautiful from afar, yet close up he found them chilly to the touch. How many years had he spent learning to live far away from the family, studying so that he wouldn't have to work all day in a supermarket and all night as a security guard like Uncle Thierno? What was the purpose of all that learning?

That's what he did, studied. Especially after his mother's death the year he started community college. He hadn't gone home for a long time after that, maybe five years, and when he did, he was just starting his second year at his first job, a job crunching numbers at a financial firm in New York, a job like the kind you see on TV. He wore a suit and a crisp yellow silk tie. He read the *Wall Street Journal* and marvelled at the fresh flowers in the reception area on the 49th floor where his cubicle was. He knew that the cost of that daily bouquet could feed a family of five for a month in half the world's poorest countries. He actually sat down to do the calculations. Late at night, after working all day, waiting for the car-service company to call him and tell him that some Eastern European immigrant driver was downstairs at the firm's fancy entrance, waiting to take him home, he would do the math. It was a simple process of translation:

He would look at exchange rates and the poverty datum lines of the poorest countries like Chad and Haiti. He had toyed with the idea of starting some kind of drive, perhaps every firm in the US could give up their daily bouquets on Fridays, and the money could go toward a food fund for the Third World.

His supervisor was underwhelmed by the idea and told him to talk to someone in HR. He sat down with a nice, blonde lady who pointed out to him how overwhelming the logistics would be, the difficulties of creating a viable operation that didn't just use the collected monies to pay off its own overheads. Discouraged, he went home and rented a DVD about New York City being blown up by aliens.

Had he changed? A vase of flowers was just that to him now. It was what it was. For him, it was too late to come home.

'I don't think Babacar would be...' again his tongue was lost in a vacuum of cultural difference, '...happy. In the long run. Fulfilled.'

Fatima drew a sharp intake of breath. Uncle Djiby bobbed his head to the music and laughed aloud. Was he laughing at him? Ibou wondered.

'Happy?' Her voice was incredulous. 'Please, Brother,' she began again, pragmatism hollowing out her words, 'When we sent you to America, it was for the good of the family. We sent you to study for us.'

'You don't understand,' he shook his head.

Us. In America, there was only me. Families met once or twice a year at the holidays. At Thanksgiving, perhaps at Christmas. They ate a big meal together and then mostly watched TV, maybe a football game, or a romantic comedy. Then they took advantage of the holiday sales. They don't pay the school fees of a dozen younger cousins, or send half their salary to their paternal uncle to distribute amongst the needier family members. They are not expected to raise an 11-year-old nephew in a one-bedroom apartment on the Upper East Side! He shook his head. 'I can't do it.'

Fatima was finally getting angry. Her feet were sweating in her best gold sandals with bronze jewels on the straps. 'But you too had the chance to go. If it wasn't for Uncle Thierno, you wouldn't be where you are now. Why are you denying Babacar the chance you were given?'

'Why can't we send him to a good school here? If he does well, he'll get into a good college in the States and I'll help out financially.'

'Even if he does very well, the competition is steep. It's better if you take him now as a child. It's hard to get student visas. *C'est difficile dé!*'

'There has to be a way.'

'You are the way!' All these years she had accompanied Ibou to and from the airport. She waited for him to arrive and then waited for his plane to take off. She waved at the disappearing jet, knowing that he could not see her out of the tiny fish-eye windows, but knowing it was her duty to wait until the plane had streamed up into another stratosphere, somewhere up near the stars. A place she would never go. Except in her mind. She must remain here because if she didn't, Maimouna sometimes joked, who would? Not everyone could be there or there would be no here. But where she couldn't go, Babacar could. And would.

'*You* are the way.'

'I can't bring him to live with us. It's impossible.'

'Please think about the family. If Babacar can earn well, he will look after the whole family.'

'This is not about the family. It's about my life. I can't sacrifice my life, our life, our privacy, our time. And Babacar won't be happy. Trust me. He should stay here and go to a good school here. It's for the best.' Then he added, without intending to, 'I can't feed half the world.'

'Why do those who profit from the kindness of others hoard their success all for themselves?' Her voice was shrill, sharp. But inside she was thinking it must be Ghada's fault: she had made Ibou more bitter than the last round of ataya.

'Are you calling me selfish? After all I do for this family when I couldn't even–'

Fatima leaned out the open window and spat to cleanse her palate. A globule of throbbing, jelly-like spit landed somewhere in the darkness. She longed desperately for water to wash away the harsh words brewing on her tongue. Exerting every last ounce of control, she said softly, 'Ibou, you are a good man, and a good brother and you have not forgotten us. What I'm asking you now is for the wellbeing of the whole family. It's only a few years until he will be old enough to live by himself. Only *you* are equipped to look after him until that time.'

Uncle Djiby braked suddenly and pulled up to the kerb. They were at the airport. All three of them got out. The luggage was placed on a rickety cart which kept veering off to the left. Ibou turned to Uncle Djiby, sticking out his hand in farewell. But Uncle Djiby's red-rimmed eyes glowed at him. 'No, no, Americain Boy, I am just going to park the car.'

'There is no need to come in,' said Ibou.

'No, no, we'll say goodbye in *la salle de départ*...' Djiby muttered, ducking back into the car.

Ibou said nothing in response but merely nodded and pushed his cart in front of the bustle of people. Fatima tried to retain a hand on the handle to show that she was being helpful but Ibou was going too fast for her. She gave up and lagged behind, smiling apologetically at the people he unconsciously brushed past. He found a place in the check-in queue and they stood there silently. He ruffled through his passport, a dark American blue, and produced the single flimsy sheet of his return e-ticket. Fatima watched him dispassionately.

'Where is Uncle Djiby?' he asked finally, breaking the silence binding them together in a knot of unspoken words. The queue was inching forward.

'He'll be here soon. He must have met some taxi driver friends of his.'

They got to the Air France counter. The man looked at

Ibou's face and then at his US passport and began hesitantly in English. Ibou answered forcefully in Wolof, '*Wa Senegal-lê* [I am Senegalese].'

'*Bien sûr*,' the man said quickly, but he answered in French, as if to underscore Ibou's compromised status. Their interaction continued in French, formal, the bare necessities of what gate to go to and the whereabouts of his baggage claim tickets.

Fatima stood to the side with his laptop and carry-on bag as he received his boarding pass. He carefully pocketed his passport and she looked speculatively at the dark blue colour. It was almost the same colour as his jeans. Should she ask him again? What to do now? Her throat was parched and words blossomed in her head and then expired on her swollen tongue.

Ibou took off his cap and wiped a palm over his shaved scalp. He replaced the cap and looked around, 'Where is Uncle Djiby?'

Fatima tried to talk but she could only nod her head. She wanted to say that he would be here any moment now but the words kept getting stuck, grazing her throat like a chicken bone. Then abruptly, she spoke but she didn't say what she had intended. Instead she said: 'I am the one who waits always and watches others come and go. I am the one who always remains behind so that you can go.'

Ibou looked at her for a long time, his eyes bright and his jaw slack, his mouth slightly open. He seemed to be panting for breath. Finally, he shook his head in incomprehension. Even Fatima wasn't sure what she had meant. It was just a feeling, a rubbery suspicion like beef fat. She could chew and chew on it but it never seemed to break down and even if she swallowed it, she wasn't sure that her intestines could digest it.

They stood there in front of the metal-detector machine, passengers and their farewell entourages bidding them *bon voyage*, jostling them on all sides. There were garbled announcements over the PA system. The whole world seemed to be vibrating except for the two of them, a brother and a sister – still locked in the circle of their own impasse.

She knew she could plead, she could beg, she could invoke God and their deceased mother, she might sniffle and weep and take off her foulard to press against her eyes.

But she did not do this. Instead, her ring went round and round her finger, scraping her dry knuckle an ashy white.

Time ticked. Uncle Djiby did not appear.

Ibou glanced at his watch. 'I have to go...' His voice trailed off. She could only nod.

'Goodbye,' he said. 'Thank you for everything.' Awkwardly, he embraced her rigid shoulders and then quickly turned and pushed into the crowd putting their luggage through the X-ray machine. He took his carry-on and put it on the moving belt. Then he took off his watch, his iPod and his cellphone and put them in a tray along with his laptop. He stood in front of the metal detector. When the official waved him to come forward, he stepped through the metal frame, trapped for a second on the border between his world and hers, silhouetted against the bright light of the other side. Time teetered; she held her breath. But then he was through, into a world where she would never venture. He looked back at her and lifted a hand.

Then he was gone. She would wait for his plane to take off.

Melissa Tandiwe Myambo is the author of *Jacaranda Journals* (Macmillan South Africa, 2004: www.jacarandajournals.com), a collection of short stories set in Zimbabwe. Her short fiction has appeared in *34th Parallel*, *Chelsea Station*, the *Journal of African Travel Writing*, the *Montréal Review*, *Opening Spaces: An Anthology of Contemporary African Women's Writing*, *Prick of the Spindle* and *Wasafiri* (forthcoming). 'La Salle de Départ' is part of a new collection of short stories tentatively entitled *Airport Stories*.

Hunter Emmanuel
Case 1: Saws & Whores

Constance Myburgh

HUNTER EMMANUEL SHOULDERED HIS CHAINSAW and looked up at the trees.

That, he thought, is some crazy shit.

The leg hung from a branch three-quarters up the pine's trunk. It was a woman's leg, he thought, though you could never know one hundred per cent, and it had been cut off right at the crotch, at the dip he liked so much, probably his favourite place in a chick. Except for other obvious locations. No way to tell what colour it was either: the leg was smeared with grime and dirt and had started to go black. It had rained the night before. He wondered what sort of string was holding it up there.

A commotion had begun behind him. The tree was, like all the others, marked with a great yellow 'X', so it had to come down. But the leg posed a problem. The foreman was deciding whether to send one of the guys up to get it down, or whether to chop the tree and then deal with it.

'That's 15 metres of solid pine,' someone said.

'Has anyone called the police?'

Elsewhere in the shrinking woods, a hundred-year-old alien crashed to the ground.

A woman's leg, hanging from the tallest tree in a doomed forest.

Hunter Emmanuel turned his back on it.

'Fok this shit,' he said, mainly to himself. 'I'm going home.'
At his interview three weeks ago, Emmanuel had said he was
good at cutting things up. Only in this country, he thought
now, would a crack like that actually get him the job. He sat
on a squeaking armchair in the contractor's office, really just
a container. What was he doing here? At least there was free
coffee. He always took extra sugar when it was free. If it was
free, you had to take it. Just like when you're down on your
luck, there's always someone with a bright idea. In this case,
he'd heard from a chommie that this company had been
awarded some government contract to cut down the alien
pines in Cecilia Forest. They'd be looking for lumberjacks,
no questions asked. Why not? Emmanuel had thought at the
time. He couldn't have known how many fokkin pine trees
there could be on one mountain.

Now he was waiting for the cops to have their turn with
him. If he could choose, if he ever had a choice, he'd rather
be anywhere else in the entire world.

'Hunter,' said Sgt Williams, 'we've missed you.'

It took all his self-control to stop Emmanuel vomiting into
his cup. The coffee was too fokkin sweet.

He recognized some of these blue assholes. The ones here
must've been those who couldn't cut it. All the other *ous* he'd
trained with would be promoted by now. These were just the
professional sidekicks.

Sgt Williams continued, 'So. This leg. You see anything
suspicious?'

'Yes,' said Emmanuel, 'I saw the leg.'

Williams leaned forward. 'Hunter. I expect more from
someone with, uh, a background in the force.'

Emmanuel didn't know how to answer this one. There
were just too many possibilities.

'We can make life difficult for you, you know?' said the Sgt,
leaning back to her original position.

'You already have.'

Was it really right, he wondered, for a woman to look like that, if there was anything she could do about it?

'But you gave us no choice, *seun.*'

That was true, conceded Emmanuel. That was the *bliksem* of it all.

Afterwards he stood outside the container, smoking. He was starving. He had a lunchbox with him, but was much too depressed to open it now. A telephone rang inside. Black clouds were gathering on the mountain, but Emmanuel couldn't tell whether they meant rain, or were just faking. Either way, he knew the wind would howl tonight.

He turned his face away when the cops left the office. Sgt Williams ignored him. She'd had her fun, and she now seemed to be lost in thought. Emmanuel knew the look. He grabbed one of the boys in blue, the one last to leave the container, like the weakest wildebeest. The cop looked startled. He had a woman's eyes. He wouldn't last five minutes.

'What news did Williams get just now? What lead is there?'

'They found the woman.'

'Woman?'

'The one from who the leg's from.'

'Hospital?'

'Groote Schuur.'

The cop pulled away, but Emmanuel tightened his grip.

'Nice try. They won't let me in without a name.'

'Zara something... Zara Swart.'

Emmanuel freed the cop.

'Anything else? The name's familiar.'

'Why should I tell you?'

Emmanuel shoved his thumb into the cop's eye.

'Fok, man! The name *is* familiar. She's a fokkin whore.'

A one-legged whore. Friday nights didn't get better than this, thought Emmanuel as he walked up to Groote Schuur from

Main Road. He'd wanted to give Williams enough time to make her own enquiries, but if he left it any longer he'd be pushing visiting hours. He walked through the glass doors, swallowing hard on the smells of pathos and piss.

He didn't know the *slet*'s age, so he played safe and told the receptionist he was Swart, Zara's cousin. What would this receptionist woman know? She looked like Sgt Williams.

'Where did they find her?' he asked.

'Out at Hout Bay docks,' replied the receptionist, with only the vaguest hint of pleasure. 'When they were feeding the seals, throwing the bits of fish to them. I hear that's when they found her.'

Zara Swart wasn't hard to find: the only decent-looking thing in the ward with a missing leg, cut off right there by the hip. Not the kind of whore he'd last seen on the street, the ones he'd left with faces stewing in alcohol. She was still fresh, this one, at least to his eyes. Maybe he'd seen her before, he couldn't tell without the make-up. They must have pumped her full of drugs for the pain, so she didn't stir at his arrival. Knocked out. Saliva had drooled out of the corner of her mouth and dried on her chin. Something made him reach out to wipe it away. Maybe because she looked like someone, someone he could talk to. Maybe.

Zara Swart jumped awake at his touch. She looked washed-out, but after what she'd been through, who wouldn't be? Also, she was, he thought, probably prettier that way.

He sat down next to her and placed the flowers he'd picked on the side of the highway on the bedside table.

'I don't know you,' she said to him.

'Maybe,' answered Emmanuel. 'But I want to know what your other leg was doing dangling from a pine tree, while you were taking a swim on the other side of town.'

'You don't look like a cop.' The world could be ending, but trust a woman to always have some suspicion handy to throw in your face like a wet *lap*.

'I'm undercover.'

'The police was here already.'

Emmanuel changed tack.

'OK. I'll be straight with you. I'm not police. I'm not anything. I'm just interested. These things interest me. So, you don't have to tell me a bloody thing. But you will.'

'Why?'

'Because everyone wants to tell their story.'

She stared at him.

'I don't remember anything.'

'Someone cut off my leg, that's something I'd remember.'

'The police are already –'

'You think the police are going to solve this one? You're a whore. That's already bad. But you're also a whore that's still alive. That's worse. If you were dead, there'd be more chance they'd give a shit.'

'And you do?'

He leaned closer to her, he couldn't help it.

'I was there. I found your leg. That shit is traumatizing. I need closure.'

He loved those words. They made sense, even when they didn't.

'What… what did it look like?'

Her eyes were wide.

'I won't lie, it wasn't pretty.'

She sighed. 'It wasn't supposed to…'

'What wasn't?'

But she'd shut up like a clam. He'd blown it again.

'Come on. Give me a clue, sis. I swear, I'll leave you alone.'

'Like what?'

'Like, you work the docks?'

'*Ja.*'

'Where they found you?'

'*Ja.*'

'The sailors, they –'

'You've got your clue.'

'OK, OK.'

What did she mean, 'It wasn't supposed to –'? He tried not to let his eyes stray to those bandages.

Outside, he opened his lunchbox and looked for a moment at the leftover *bobotie* Aunt Faranaaz had packed for him that morning before the sun was up. He'd promised himself he wouldn't eat it, but once he'd started he didn't stop until the plastic was licked clean.

That night Hunter Emmanuel dreamt of corridors and mermaids, of seal women. Trees that stretched on and on, up and up, trunks wider than ten men's arms could reach around. Solid pine. It was no good. He'd spent enough nights similarly to know he couldn't sleep like this. He got up from the couch, quietly, so as not to wake Aunt Faranaaz, and slipped her car-keys from their hook. She was the only woman in the street to own a car; the Toyota was her pride and joy. He'd have to make sure he was back before dawn, as she left early to fetch the flowers she sold in Adderly St. He'd also have to top up the tank. He knew she watched the meter like a hawk.

He didn't know what ghosts led him back to the forest, steered his hands on the wheel, his feet on the path, off the path. Soon he was walking only on needles, but the same ghosts still swirled around him. It had been blacker than black, when he first arrived. No. It was like the blackness under his fingernails at the end of each week: gritty, composed of many things he didn't understand. But it had voices, this darkness, it spoke, and as Hunter Emmanuel collapsed to his knees, he began to see the lights. They swished past him, he tried to grab at them, but he was always too slow, suspended, too mortal. The lights were yellow, orange, there a red one, and they moved like the wind. Before he knew it he was in darkness and silence again, only the smell of the wet earth, of things changing their nature as they broke down, decomposed, only that sense remained to mark the fact that he was still alive, a part of the living world, and not some phantom in a dream other than his own.

The chainsaws woke him up. Lights flashed in his eyes, yellow, orange. Shit. They must have started cutting the trees again. Which meant he was late. Which meant it was very possible he was fired. The world suddenly seemed very unpleasant, and Emmanuel had to imagine Zara Swart's face and also her bandages from many different angles before it began to feel like a place he could deal with or accept that he was stuck in. There were two paths. One led down the mountain, to the chainsaws, to the cutting. The other led up, away from it, to somewhere else. In a few seconds he was up and walking. These kinds of decisions were never hard for him to make.

He passed some rich people, walking their dogs. He looked down at the bastardized little animals, all curls and short legs. Fok they were sad as hell. But they made him feel lonely. He passed the bleeding stumps of the trees they'd cut the day before. He wondered how different it would look if a bomb had been dropped on the forest. He turned his gaze up to one of the remaining giants, and only just restrained himself from asking what it thought of this whole fokkin mess. Instead, he looked past it, to the shadows on the slope. He shivered, and what sympathy he had for the place disappeared. No wonder bad things happened here. Those shadows were too old, too evil to be allowed in the world. For that reason alone, the forest had to go.

Higher up, a clearing had been made among the needles. It was human-made, but didn't look like the work of the men below. No, this had been done with too much care: smooth hillocks had been built up between the trees, paths were discernible, and there was something else. Hunter Emmanuel crouched down to examine the snake-like tracks that criss-crossed – now he was looking for them – almost everywhere in this quiet place. It was then it occurred to him what the lights – last night, so they were real – what the lights he had seen could belong to. He felt stupid, until something else caught his eye. There in the mud, among the needles and bits of bark, there it was: a woman's fingernail, manicured with that white line at the top, but now going greyish, cracked in places. Hunter Emmanuel stared at it for a moment, before putting it in his pocket. Even from there, out of sight, he felt cursed by it, as if, along with the shadows, that nail was the source of all evil.

He still had time. When he returned with the things he would need, the sun was only starting to go down. He was glad he'd brought supplies even if it'd used the last of his cash. OK, not quite the last. There was always Faranaaz's petrol to consider, if he ever had the balls to take the car back. When it finally had become dark he'd already strung the very thin wire as tight as he could between the trees. He could sit and eat his Nik-Naks in peace, and wait. He doubted the wire would stop them all, but he was pretty sure he'd get at least one of them. One would be enough.

Just as his eyes were closing, he heard the needles crunching, slithering. Voices. The ghosts had arrived. Then, as he expected, a crash. There were shouts, and then, silence again, except for a pathetic whimpering sound. Hunter Emmanuel's heart almost went out to the kid, sprawled in the mud of the bike-track, his fallen bicycle twisted under him, his friends long gone. There it was, the flashing safety light, strapped to the back of the bicycle. These kids. Their parents really did care about them. Emmanuel put out a hand to help him up, but the white boy jumped away. He was younger than expected, maybe 11, 12, you could never tell. He'd grazed his knee and hands badly in the fall. Emmanuel knew that feeling, how it must be burning. But now was no time for sympathy. Anyway, the kid spoke first.

'Please don't kill me.'

'*Laaitie*, just because I'm not white, doesn't mean…'

Now was no time for that either.

'Look. I'm a policeman.' He flashed the card. It was too dark for the kid to see it was the old ID from when he worked as security for Pick n Pay.

'You know that leg they found, here, in the forest? You know what I'm talking about?'

The kid was still too scared, in too much shock, in too much pain, to speak.

'Your friends, they've gone. They're not here to answer my questions. But you are.'

He knew one good *klap* would get the truth out in no time, but he was trying so hard, so hard not to be a bad guy.

'I know you kids found that leg. I know it was here.'

The boy was picking dirt out of his cut hands, but Emmanuel knew he was thinking.

'You know they send kids to jail too? You know what they do there, don't you?'

'We thought it was funny.'

'You what?'

'Funny. We thought it was funny.'

'What was so funny?'

'It wasn't my idea.'

'What wasn't your idea?' Fok, this was tiresome.

'To hang it up there. We just found it, and then…'

'You hung the leg, up there, in the tree? You thought it was funny to hang a human leg from a tree?'

'But it wasn't real. It wasn't a real leg.'

The kid looked at him strangely – surely not, was it scorn?

'*Ja* no sure, it wasn't a real leg. Of course. Now *voetsek*.'

The kid picked up his bike, testing the wheel alignment with frightening professionalism.

'Go find your little friends.'

The kid looked back, and yes, it was scorn in his face.

'There are criminals, like robbers and murderers and stuff.

They were here that night. We scared them away.' A pause. 'Our security people saw them, but they got away, because they were covered in Vaseline or something. Criminals and… You're police, why can't you fucking catch them?'

Yes, there were criminals everywhere, thought Hunter Emmanuel as he watched the kid limp off, pushing his bike. Criminals everywhere.

Sun-up he was at the Hout Bay docks.

'There. That's where they found her.'

The dock-worker wore a cap that even in the pale morning light cast his eyes into shade. His stomach was huge, his legs like toothpicks. He looked like a canapé, of cheese and pineapple, like Emmanuel'd seen once at someone's wedding.

He was pointing at the edge of the pier, where the seals batted at jellyfish or plastic packets in the filthy water.

'You know her? I hear she worked around here?'

The dock-worker shook his head.

'No, man. Ask the girls. She wasn't one of ours.'

He gestured over to the fish and chip shop, where a cluster of tired whores smoked morning cigarettes on the damp benches, salty from the last night's sea fog. They must smell like diesel and fish, he thought. Sweat and cigarettes.

Zara Swart didn't smell like that. He should have known the bitch would lie to him.

The man was looking down into the water, as if divining some future in the oily rainbows.

'Whoever it was, they did that *slet* a favour.'

'That you'll have to explain to me.'

The man scrutinized him from beneath his cap, through his blindfold of shadow.

'You out there on the boats, you hurt yourself. You hurt yourself bad, and it happens. But if it's winter, then you lucky.'

'Oh *ja*?'

'You hurt, you bleeding, but you too far away to get help.

But in winter, the sea, she's cold. Like ice. Stops the bleeding till you get back to land.'

That's good, that's very good, thought Hunter Emmanuel as he walked away. Zara Swart might be a lying whore, but whoever it was that cut her leg off dumped her in the sea. There among the fish heads and the seals, where she'd be found, short one leg, but with some blood left in her veins. Someone wanted to teach her a lesson, get rid of her, shut her up, maybe. But they hadn't wanted her dead.

He didn't care that it was a hospital, he was going to give her a piece of his mind. But when he got there, Zara Swart was asleep again. Mouth open as before. What a sight. A sorry sight. He was as sorry as hell. Instead he looked at her hands, both of which were above the covers, like a Virgin Mary's. Open hands, no weapons. Just like a woman, open hands. The nurses hadn't removed Zara Swart's false nails. Probably knew how much it must have cost her to have them done. They were all there, just as he expected, yes, except one. He reached into his pocket and brought out the piece of chipped plastic. Still, no doubt. It was from the same hand. The real nail, on Zara Swart's naked finger, was bitten, bitten right down. He could see why she had been forced to get them done up. Good-looking fingers are important in a whore. But what did this mean? Biting her nails? She was nervous, worried about something. One thing? Or was she always worried? He needed to know more about Zara Swart. He needed her to let him in. Inside, that's where he could save her. But how could he get there? He looked at her sleeping, and imagined he could crawl inside her, through her open mouth. And now he remembered who she reminded him of. She looked like his first girlfriend, Christine, who he hadn't thought about in years. He remembered now, that day they first got together, how they spent the whole afternoon, sitting on his parents' couch, kissing. The next day, he'd gone to school, he'd been so proud. He told all his friends what he'd done, how he'd kissed Christine for at least three hours. His friends had all laughed at him and he hadn't spoken to Christine again. Fok, yes, he needed to know more about Zara Swart, so he stole her bag from the bedside table. She'd left it unlocked, so it was her own bloody fault anyway. Didn't she know that hospitals were dangerous places? Fokkin dangerous. People died there all the time.

He let himself into her room with her keys. The place was in Salt River, and fok, it was a shithole. But who was he to be snobby? He didn't even have a room of his own. Still, he could imagine her sitting there, in the afternoons, staring at that brown ceiling, wanting, willing to do anything, for something else, other than this. Yes, was beyond doubt. He agreed with her, this vision of her in his mind. She was better than this. He was hoping to avoid the situation, but eventually, he was forced to, took a piss in her bathroom. Standing there, he wondered how many other men had stood where he was, for how long, and... He cast his eyes around, over the few things she owned. She was a neat girl, that he could say for her – it was easier to be neat when you were poor. But there was one thing, one thing that didn't belong. On the kitchen counter was a flyer. Not much writing on it, just simply:

We Buy Gold

And a phone number.

This couldn't be right. Whatever she was like inside, Zara Swart was a whore, and whores didn't have gold. He looked around, in drawers, places she'd hide things. No, there was none, nothing other than a few rings and bracelets that even he could tell were fake. There was no gold. Unless she'd already sold it? No. No, he couldn't believe it. But if that was true, why keep this flyer? Why keep it when nowhere else was there anything extra, anything not in its proper place? There was only one way to find out. Yes, there was. But first he needed airtime.

At the nearest Caltex he punched in the secret, individual, special, one-time airtime code and watched the black guys rip off the lone coloured petrol attendant with diamonds in his front teeth. That ritual accomplished, Emmanuel dialled the number on the flyer and cleared his throat. Be prepared, fokkin prepared. That was his motto.

A man answered.

'Hello?'

'I hear you buy.'

'You want to sell? Gold?'

'I want to sell… the other thing.'

Hunter Emmanuel waited.

'Man or woman?'

How best to answer this?

'Woman.'

'Good. Be at the dry docks, the pier at B6. One a.m.'

'How much?'

'It depends what. You can expect at least 6,000. We will take care of everything.'

At last, thought Hunter Emmanuel as he pocketed his phone and stepped back into rush-hour traffic. At last. Progress.

He was early. He wanted to look around. He walked the length of pier B6, passing the ships docked there, listening, always listening. Several Chinese sailors strolled by, eating ice-creams. Other than that, and birdsong coming from the hold of a dark ship, no sign of life. It was 12:45 when he saw it. Stuck to a pole, a piece of paper: **We Buy Gold**. Hunter Emmanuel stopped at the end of the pier and looked out to sea. It was dark out there, dark and cold, that he knew. He couldn't imagine what Zara Swart had been doing here, if she had been here at all. Had she called the number? And if she had, what was she selling? It wasn't as if she had much to…

It's always unsatisfying, when just as you're about to connect the dots, someone hits you over the head, very hard, with what feels like a fokkin spanner.

Hunter Emmanuel crumpled to the ground, not quite out yet, he grabs, grabs at whoever has attacked him. Once again, he is too slow. His hands touch something slimy, something slippery. Vaseline.

Fok, thinks Hunter Emmanuel, as the world goes even darker than it was before.

Sgt Williams was leaning over him.

'Hunter,' she said, 'what's your problem, hey?'

Finally, he thought. A good question.

He was in hospital. But which hospital?

'Where am I?'

'Groote Schuur. You've been out for a week.'

Crazy shit, thought Hunter Emmanuel. That is crazy shit.

'You'll be glad to know your girlfriend's better. Zara. She's just leaving.'

He was too fast for Sgt Williams. Too fast for anyone. Too fast for her.

He caught Zara Swart as she was wheeling herself out of the hospital doors.

'Why did you do it?'

She turned, her hands on the bars of the wheelchair. He couldn't help it. He looked at her leg, the one they'd let her keep.

'Why did I do what?'

'Sell your leg. Sell it, I don't know why, I don't know who buys it or why, but this world is fucked up, I know that, it is so fucked up we can't even understand it, but – I know you did it.'

He didn't realize her eyes were made of steel. He had her attention, but fok, it hurt.

'Just tell me. Just tell me I'm right. Just, I want to understand.'

Zara Swart chose her words carefully, just like she chose everything.

'What I want to understand, is why you need to know?'

He had a million answers. He had no answers. He had one answer.

'A man must investigate. It's in a man's soul to investigate.'

'You men,' said Zara Swart, 'you always think you can fokkin save us.'

She was already wheeling herself down to Main Road by the time his eyes cleared. He called after her.

'Something is happening,' his voice sounded strange, 'but I don't know what it is!'

The wind was on her side now. It whisked his words away and helped her, pushed her, away from him.

'You don't know anything about women, Hunter.' Sgt Williams was behind him.

He wasn't going to reply to that. He was never going to reply to anything again.

Why was he here? He was so sure this would all end back in the forest, that whatever trail of blood he'd find would lead back to the shadows there. And yet here he was. On a fokkin street corner on Main Road. No, it was as he feared. The shadow was everywhere.

'Come back inside, Hunter. You look like you need some help.' Sgt Williams put a heavy hand on his shoulder.

No. No help. He needed a new job. He needed... maybe he must just buy a dog, he thought, as he allowed her to steer him back, into the mouth of Groote Schuur. A man must investigate. Without investigation he is nothing.

If it wasn't for the fact that I can't even solve my own fokkin life, thought Hunter Emmanuel, I could make a best-ever, real-life, private investigator.

Jenna Bass, writing as **Constance Myburgh**, is a South African film-maker, photographer, writer and retired magician. Her award-winning, Zimbabwe-set short film, *The Tunnel*, premiered at the Sundance and Berlin Film Festivals and continues to screen internationally. She is currently engaged on her debut feature, *Tok Tokkie*, a supernatural noir set in Cape Town. Jenna is also the editor and co-creator of *Jungle Jim*, a pulp-literary magazine for African writing.

The Caine Prize
African Writers' Workshop Stories 2012

Elephants Chained to Big Kennels

Mehul Gohil

CEPHAS STANDS ON THE ROOF, where streaming warmth catches his face and seeps into his cheeks. There is a race in the sky between the rising sun and the cloudwall of the Kenyan monsoon. It's an April dawn and he is calculating how many minutes before the rain creates a jam on Landhies Road. There is only the cool and fast wind blowing south-west and not even a drizzle yet to breathe in. And this is all he sees because he doesn't want to angle his face either level or downward.

It's the rare moment when there is a windhowl warping around his ears and the chaos at street level has fallen silent for a minute. And this is his last second to look directly at it, the sun, and see the outline of its circle of fire and the wash of its corona. He lets it burn his iris and lets his pupil take the brilliant light deep into his head and he thinks he can feel his brain fluids come to a bubbling boil. He hears an airplane breaking the barrier somewhere in the sky.

The cloudwall eats the sun and the light goes out of his eyes and he sees them clearly, the greys of the approaching storm. Long rains and floods and muddy socks in the Omo foam. The wind becomes cooler and now he thinks he can taste it like ice-cream.

'That's why you can't read your own handwriting.'

This is his brother Erabus' voice. And how does he know

Erabus is standing six feet tall on the ground, not looking at him, but looking down at his iPhone? It's because all he needs to hear is the modulation that hits 'you can't' after the 'why' and the neck bend is on, and the voiceless breath between 'hand' and 'writing' that indicates he is distracted by finger moves over a keyboard. This knowledge comes from seven years of watching Erabus play the single-parent and only brother.

'Don't mind my iris. Did you take the day off because you want to be shown the cloud downtown?' Cephas asks his brother.

'Look, ask me your questions.'

This is the signal for Cephas to play the game where little brother becomes the teacher and big brother the student.

'Did you buy the tickets?'

'No. But I tried.'

Cephas jumps off the wall like the city spider that he is, landing asprawl, hands and feet hitting the ground simultaneously, smoky dust rising around his sneakers; without breaking his bones because he's just a kid enjoying the rubberbandiness of his body.

He stands up and sees the city and its downtown jungle of skyscrapers.

'How is downtown shaped?' asks Cephas.

'Like a grown lady lying on her back. From left to right, from here, we have her thighs which are the squat buildings on Haile Selassie. Except for the raised knees which are Co-operative House and Times Tower. The flat stomach of Moi Avenue and Tom Mboya Street after that. Then the rising breasts of Johnny Walker on Teleposta Towers. Finally, we go down to her head which is Tusker on Uhuru Flyover.'

This is how Cephas reads the city. He takes the five biggest billboards in downtown and makes them his map.

First, a hundred metres down Landhies Road, where he now stands, is Blueband. It has a boy like him eating his slice of buttered bread. A male billboard he calls a *he*.

'You said you tried?'

'Yes. See for yourself.'

Underneath Blueband, Cephas sees the trails his brother has left on dust caking the tarmac. Erabus walks in slides and not steps. And Cephas makes out the route he took, the trails leading to Machakos Bus Station where he sees slides tracing the ground from the Naivasha matatus to the Nakuru matatus to the Eldoret matatus and onward to the Turkana ones.

And he sees the witch called Aeron selling her books from the back of her blue matatu, and she's wearing a bikini but it is legal and she knows the City Council bastards don't want to touch her wrinkly skin or fondle her sagging breasts, and he catches a line of her bipolar monologue booming from the matatu stereo, 'There is light in the darkness, but the darkness does not understand it.'

Then, still going straight along Landhies Road to where it merges into Haile Selassie Avenue, the eastern edge of downtown, there is the looming Airtel which has a girl calling her mother on her iPhone. He calls her a *she*. And she casts a shadow on the yellow wall of bananas marking the boundary of Wakulima Market. Past gaps in the wall there are muscular women lifting LG flatscreens and putting them on the stall tables.

At the entrance to the downtown proper, just to the right of Haile Selassie Avenue, is the Coca-Cola billboard.

'The lady drinking the Coca-Cola has what?'

'She has curves just the way a grown man would want to see them.'

Coca-Cola is a *she*.

Then, in a diagonal line westward from Coca-Cola there is the looming Johnny Walker billboard on Teleposta Towers. The Teleposta Towers has three faces to it and each one has Johnny Walker on it. Cephas knows when he is in the heart of downtown Johnny Walker is always looking down on him. And it's a male.

When you go past Johnny Walker you are going beyond

downtown and westward out of Nairobi and the Tusker billboard flies over Uhuru Flyover.

These billboards are his compass points. As long as they are there, he can't get lost.

'So now?' says Cephas.

'We try Aeron.'

'And when we get to the Rift Valley, it will look just like you said?'

'Yes. It's too big to change.'

Cephas sees Erabus take out his iPhone and he doesn't like that.

'I thought you said you were taking a day off. Now you are taking out your office,' says Cephas.

Erabus puts the iPhone back into his pocket.

'Cloud of newspapers,' says Erabus out of his nose.

Cephas squints both his eyes and points a finger up at Erabus' face.

'Wait until you see it to know what bullshit you are,' Cephas tells his brother.

A gang of men and women dressed in power suits and even more powerful skirts come out of their houses lined up on Landhies Road and they walk like they are a common army. They are walking to downtown, from Blueband to Coca-Cola, and Cephas gets the nervous feeling that he and Erabus are in their way. He can smell their aftershave and white-collar perfume.

And they are all looking down into their iPhones.

And it's perhaps a coincidence. The Kenyan monsoon winds flow toward downtown, the traffic on Landhies Road swims toward downtown and the power suits and even more powerful skirts walk toward downtown and what is this downtown? Cephas and Erabus turn and walk briskly, as if to make a getaway or at least stay ahead of the aftershave and perfume pack and they see the Times Towering giants and concrete sequoias rising to the sky, Co-operative House and Afya House.

Cephas bumps his knee onto a bench. An old bench.

'Who sat on this once?' asks Cephas, rubbing his knee.

'Grandfather sat on it and looked out to a sprawling green field where there were stumps at the wicket and the Englishmen played cricket.'

The construction companies forgot about the bench and it sat looking at the dirty white walls of the houses on Landhies Road.

They come to Aeron's blue matatu.

'Any hardcover, any time, anywhere in my matatu at a hundred shillings,' her voice booms out of the matatu stereo.

Her skin matters to everyone standing around the back of her matatu.

'This is elephant skin.'

'It's like looking down at a swath of wrinkly grey Ethiopian mountains from an airplane window.'

There are many here, at the open back of Aeron's blue matatu where used hard and softcovers are stacked, and it seems books are popular and maybe this is a reading city. An ex-power skirt is flipping to a last page. There are thin men with big bones, the underfed and underpaid houseboys from deeper Eastlands, stopping here at Aeron's and flipping the softcover pages for a minute before continuing their trek to the middle-class suburbs where they will scrub chicken tikka stains off plates and wash shit-farted underwears. The monsoon wind billows their baggy pants. And the fat man in the faded Omo-blue jeans, which he's about to tear at thigh-level, cradles a softcover with one hand and flips a hard one to the last page with the other. Aeron digs into her sagging left breast and takes out an iPhone.

'Any time, anywhere, a hundred shillings. Or softcover me at half price, but I will not take off my costume,' Aeron's voice booms.

Cephas grabs Erabus' arm.

'Give her the money. Buy them now,' Cephas says, pulling on Erabus' hands.

'Aeron, give us two "Out of Africa" tour tickets,' says Erabus.

Aeron digs into her right sagging breast and takes out two tickets, hands them over to Erabus.

'Since this young boy is a spider, I will not charge. And I need to give him something.'

Aeron crawls into the back of her matutu, showing off her elephant skin rump. She comes out with a dirty, old book. Cephas grabs it. The pages look like they can easily fall off. Bold black title on the white hardcover spells out **Human Evolution**. He checks out the inside jacket.

'What does it say?' Cephas asks, giving the book to Erabus.

'A cracking and suspenseful thriller of our history based on brand new science. Filled with CG photos and an updated map of our trip out of Africa with exact town locations in the Great Rift Valley. By the obscure American author Olliled Nod,' reads Erabus.

Aeron then lifts a softcover that looks more like a loose-leaf pad and shows it to Erabus. The softcover is grubby and Erabus can smell the whiff of a wine on the corner of the cover because it is now under his nose.

'That's a 110-year-old Eselshoek. Mugabe was drinking it in his toilet,' says Aeron.

Erabus wants to lean away from the book but he can't because there is a moving mass of Nairobi bodies blocking his retreat. Cephas spies the power suits and even more powerful skirts army approaching and he sees a title typed on the soft cover, **A Sunrise on a Murderous Day in Kampala**.

'By Dambooze Marechera. Yeah, baby, his last book never published. This only manuscript stolen from Mugabe's toilet. And these are his fingerprints,' Aeron says as she shows the finger stains to everyone.

'He held it in his lap as he shat. This is how Marechera wanted his books read. While performing raw human arts like shitting. Fine alcohol ready at hand. Bob was always an avid reader.'

Suddenly, there is a push on Cephas and he dominoes into Erabus, who spills into Aeron, and the three of them tumble and Erabus licks sweat on Aeron's armpits. A foot of power suit stamps on Cephas' knee but the spider in him wriggles out. The power suit's boot hits the ground and he loses balance. The even more powerful skirt next to him starts to wobble as the gyroscopic forces holding her five-inch stiletto heels in place are neutralized and she does something out of kung-fu, swinging her thighs outward, in exact and opposite directions. The slits in her even more powerful skirt part, showing the fine pink lace of her panties. She lands in some sort of eastern-religion crouch where the five-inch stilettos keep her skin and clothes from touching the ground and she remains as antiseptic and germ free as in the morning when she came out of her shower and applied perfume in front of a smoky mirror. But one of the stilettos has landed next to Aeron's arm and punctured Dambooze's book right through the middle and Aeron, who is still holding the book, instinctively tears it from the stiletto's clutch, sending feathers of paper floating low into the air.

The Kenyan monsoon clouds come and cover the blue sky. The city lives under a shadow. The wind now has a punch and is ice-cream cool.

Cephas and Erabus pass under Airtel. Downtown-bound matatus are bullying sedans – get off the road mutherfuckers. The matatus are multi-coloured and sprayed wildstyle with slogans: **Kuma Ya Aeron, Politica Landscape, Ratner's Star, Ngugi wa What? Beer Hunger Wine Hyena, Agwambo Mapambano, Jah in Fallujah, Hague Is Vague**. They have colours that shine through in this grey monsoon world – Capetown Caramel tasty on the sliding doors, Butterscotch Yellow burning around the lights and Kenya Army Green marching on the tyre rims.

'What time are we leaving?' Cephas asks his brother.

'Ticket says four o'clock in the afternoon.'

They walk into the shadow of Coca-Cola. They can't see the

outline of her shadow because it is a dark morning anyway. All the currents of humanity and vehicular reality flow into the downtown.

They are two brothers walking into downtown. A history of lost parents. Something of their father's nose or mother's lip reflects on the windows of a Bakers Inn but they cannot recognize that.

'See my hands,' Cephas shows Erabus paint-stained palms.

'You are playing with the cans again.'

'Learning my handwriting.'

Thunder cannonades from the sky but it is soon suffocated by beats blasting out from the Jesus Is Alive Ministry. People are clapping hands inside. This is the everyday religion of the city, where sinner and fucker and good guy and nice lady alike are forgiven, every day. Every building in the downtown has its sinners in some corner, like this one looking out of the 16th floor of Co-operative House, smoking something, maybe a cigar, and who knows what that means, because this is the city of Jesus Christ.

And Cephas can see Erabus hates it that he didn't spot the stained hands earlier. He's knows Erabus is losing him.

'It's like I can feel the weight of that solid ball inside the can going click-click when I see them smudged like this,' says Erabus.

'So I can't eat with these?'

Cephas puts a finger into his mouth and sucks it. The finger and tongue he sticks out gleam with spit and paint. Erabus smacks Cephas' hand away.

'What's wrong with you?'

A matatu with wild art stops in front of them. Passengers alight and the sliding door closes and they see Michael Jackson in a glimmer-jacket and there are rhinestones on his glove and he is posed with his bass weejuns on tiptoes.

'It tastes like a wild leaf in my mouth,' says Cephas, licking his lips.

They go past Coca-Cola and are now inside the jungle of

skyscrapers. They walk to Mama Ngina Street where Johnny Walker looks down on them.

The Kenyan monsoon comes crashing down. Umbrellas pop open. Those on the open pavements and roads dive under the jutting roofs of ground-floor shops and soon the entire corpus of the city is either indoors, cardoors, or standing in their five million under jutting roofs. There are flashes of iPhone screens as the five million dig into their pockets and bring them out because what else is there to do now? Fireflies in their hands in the daytime.

Cephas and Erabus are squeezed in the crowd. There is bad breath and aftershave here. Shoulders rub against each other and there is warmth in the ice-cream wind. Cephas steps out of the crowd and walks onto the road, into the rain, and in between cars which are now stuck in a jam that will be measured in half-days. He looks at the sky and what can he see. It's not grey, it's not blue, but it has headlines all over. It's black and white. They are floating in the sky. The skyscrapers are reflecting them but who knows if it's simply an optical illusion because in the crowd they are all reading the *Daily Nation* and *Standard* on their iPhones and the echo effect in the sky escapes them. Blind spot.

'**Kenyan Writer Dies of Book Hunger.**'

Cephas wants to read more headlines but an arm grabs him around the stomach and carries him back under a jutting roof. A raindrop trickles down the rim of Cephas' nose and there is an annoyance sparkling in his eye.

'Perhaps you should look up and tell me where the rain comes from,' says Cephas.

Then he hears the iPhone vibrating inside Erabus' pant pockets.

'Is there even a Rift Valley? You might be fooling me,' says Cephas.

'Look, when we get to the top of the escarpment you will be higher than 3,000-foot extinct volcanoes, peering into open craters, and not a building reflecting the stainless-steel blue sky,' says Erabus.

'When was the last time you went?' asks Cephas.

'When I was a kid like you.'

'So how do you know?'

'I told you – it's too big to change.'

'When you see the cloud of newspapers you will know what bullshit you are. I keep saying.'

Cephas is pushed by Erabus into the nearby Java. It's even warmer inside.

Cephas opens the ***Human Evolution*** book. He sees half-human, half-gorilla creatures. In big handwriting is written: '**Homo Habilis, born in Nairobi**'.

'My handwriting is much better nowadays. The other spiders respect my territory,' says Cephas.

Erabus is looking vacantly out of the big Java windows.

'Do you think they had good handwriting?' Cephas asks, pushing the book toward Erabus. Cephas looks away, trying to find a bit of sky.

'Oh yes, certainly, there is a distinct methodology in their implied process and on paper it comes out in various manifestations,' answers Erabus.

But Cephas jerks his head. This is not a pattern that fits his recognition of Erabus' voice. And he sees why. Erabus is talking into his iPhone. There is a firefly on his ear.

'I am positive, sir, I can get eight containers of cornflakes into Rwanda and your supermarkets will eat them.'

'I keep saying,' Cephas tries to grab his brother's attention.

'Sixty-seven pallets in total, sir.'

Erabus finishes the call. Cephas stands up and screams into his brother's face.

'I keep saying you never look up. None of you bastards do. You're just like them now. We'll never go, I know. Because you keep looking down at your fucking phone or anything. I am fucking gone, bro.'

* * *

Cephas chooses one of the cars parked on Mama Ngina Street, a white Toyota Immaculate, gets on top of the bonnet and reclines his back on the windscreen. The car is wet with raindrops and his clothes get soaked on the underside. But he doesn't care.

Johnny Walker is looking down on him from the cream Teleposta Towers to his right. Cephas rolls his head on the windscreen glass. He sees Coca-Cola. She looks small and red from here and home is behind her.

Mama Ngina Street, the heart of downtown. Central to everything. It has large pavements and the buildings look down at it from all sides. Power suits swarm the street like ants but here on the car he is safe from their body pushes. It's an open womb from where he observes the only world he has ever known. Erabus once told him only the lucky get out of the city because it is so big and not everyone knows where it ends. He read a Ladybird book once, a story about a boy like him who was born in a secret house on Landhies Road and went on a great journey to Mombasa so that he could see the Indian Ocean and play in its waves. The boy took matatu after matatu, going past Makindu where he ate a late breakfast at the Sikh Temple skyscraper, past Mtito Andei where elephants from Tsavo had become pets like dogs and were chained to big kennels and did not roam free in the wild grass. The boy only saw straight lines and geometric shapes of modern architecture for all those kilometres and even the trees were carefully manicured. When the boy got to Mombasa he was told the beaches had all been privatized. Out of mischief, the boy climbed over the wall of a private beach bungalow and saw an Indian Ocean without waves. There was a signpost on the sand which said: 'To Mumbai. 4439 km. Drive Safely.' It was no longer an ocean of water but an ocean of skyscrapers and cities. He saw bulbs twinkling like baby novas on the horizon. The sun never set. The water was only in between the different buildings and it was still and filled with mosquito larvae. Then the boy met a witch on the narrowest lane in Old Mombasa and she told him his journey had evolved in the wrong direction and she said something about light and darkness. She gave him a book called **Human Evolution**. 'Dear spider, the map to get out of here is inside,' she said.

But Erabus had that book with him, a little down the street, at Java. Cephas knew his big brother would not come after him now that he was negotiating his cornflakes deal. There were shortcuts through Tom Mboya that came out directly underneath Coca-Cola and around Haile Selassie there were wormholes which came out under Blue Band and home was then next door. Erabus knows little brother has a complete mastery of these tricks of folding space. And how does Cephas get his food? Like, was he hungry now? Cephas is a city spider, if he knows the wormholes, he knows where in Wakulima market the tastiest rolex can be had. And the spiders never pay.

The Toyota Immaculate's wipers scratch his back. Mama Ngina Street is jammed and there is an unceasing engine purr. Cars are stuck in first gear.

Cephas rolls his head and sees the cloud of newspapers.

It's a black and white sky. A cloud called '**Africa Faces E-Book Crises, Warns Oxfam**' crawls from Johnny Walker to Tusker and disappears. Now many clouds float in from what he thinks is the sky area around Airtel. They come and occupy the sky in rows and columns. He can see them slowly drifting south-west, being pushed on by the Kenyan monsoon winds. And he doesn't think it is exactly black or white. Instead there seems to be a luminous backlight switched on behind the clouds, giving them a digital feel, like on Erabus' iPhone. The cloud right opposite him now is called '**Ocampo Four Given Life Sentences**'. Southward there is '**Police Raid *So What?* Publishers, Find Illegal Fiction**'. The entire sky is now carpeted with newspapers and headlines. The clouds drift peacefully. '**Agwambo: I Will Expand Cities in Ukambani**' is reflecting off Lonhro House. There are geometric shadows of letters being cast on Teleposta Towers and Johnny Walker. Around Airtel, eastward, there is the glint of white space shining off Times Tower. And Cephas wonders if this is why he never goes to school. He learns just by lying down like this on a car downtown and reading whatever there is in the sky. Only his handwriting is bad. He's never held a pen and whenever he tries, his fingers get confused and it drops out of his hand. Erabus told him he had the same problem with chopsticks. But a spray can is a toy in his hands.

'**Handwriting Experts Quizzed Over Graffiti Menace.**'

'Can you please get off my car?' a sweet, well-modulated voice says. Cephas thinks he can taste spearmint in that voice. He continues to watch the clouds.

'**Reader Found Guilty Of Possessing Softcovers in Contravention of Save The Trees Act.**'

He wonders how the clouds of newspaper are formed. Do books evaporate? Does it rain in letters?

And then his spider sense tickles him. He just swings his left foot away in time and a baton comes crashing down on the Toyota Immaculate bonnet. The car's alarm goes off.

'Not the car, please'

'Don't worry, madam.'

'Please.'

City Council bastards are shouting over the alarm noise. Cephas leans forward, his wet back peels off the windscreen like a sticker, and then he stands up and towers over everybody. He wants to jump off and make a run toward Moi Avenue, which is the one gap there is in the wall of skyscrapers surrounding him, but three City Council bastards dressed in their unmistakable yellow aprons block his way. Cephas turns to see if he can rocket away in the opposite direction, toward Johnny Walker, but there are bastards in yellow aprons waiting for him there too. This is when he smells gasoline in the air and feels a bass thump beating under his feet and knows it cannot be the alarm.

'We have you by the balls, spider.'

The City Council bastards close in from all directions with some remaining just a little behind, in case he jumps over. The jam on Mama Ngina Street is static and the occupants inside take time off from their iPhones to watch the noose tightening on a spider; something for them to chew on because the digital boredom and monotony makes their minds hungry.

'Pray to Buddha, boy.'

Cephas' legs don't have a muscle memory for this fix. And he knows Erabus is not going to come out of Java because the cornflakes are stuck at Uganda border control.

And then there is a tumult at the end of Mama Ngina Street where a further road leads toward Johnny Walker. There is something blue crashing forward. Grey smoke is spewing from its exhaust, there is a new jack swing rhythm booming in the air and it becomes clear the blue thing is a matatu.

The City Council bastards are distracted and their yellow aprons flutter in sync with the booming rhythm. A chance for Cephas to spider away but he is transfixed too.

The matatu is gleaming with Omo-blue and polished silver chrome and it wants to get onto the pavement but a Toyota Flawless is in the way, so the beast attacks, sparks fly where their metal meets, the left headlight of the Toyota Flawless pops out and dangles just above road level, its windscreen shatters and glass pebbles bounce on the pavement. The blue matatu shoves the Toyota Flawless aside and comes toward Cephas.

'Get in, spider.'

At the wheels is the witch Aeron who opens the passenger door. She is smoking a cigarette and ash is falling on the bikini straps holding up her infamous sagging breasts. Cephas has no time to read the slogan emblazoned on the matatu body.

He jumps off the Toyota Immaculate's bonnet, flies over a City Council bastard, lands single-footed on the pavement, and with another leap falls into the passenger seat next to Aeron. Music splits the air. He closes the door and the matatu roars.

Aeron manoeuvres around cars, taking instant right-angled turns, aiming for the gap that leads into Moi Avenue. She turns down the music and kills the bass stereo.

'You have been reading the book you bought from me today morning?'

'No. I left it with my brother.'

'What?'

There is an urgency in Aeron's voice. She drives faster just like that. He feels himself press into the seat cushion. Tom Mboya waves a hello to them from his statue.

They come onto Landhies Road. The cloud of newspapers is no longer in the sky. There is a break in the sky and the sun shines. The next dark cloud is on the horizon.

Cephas nears home. There are people boarding matatus at Machakos Bus Station. He too is going out of this city tonight. Erabus has the tickets.

'Is one of your matatus taking us away at four o'clock?' asks Cephas.

'This very one.'

They arrive just outside their house. The old bench stands opposite the white walls.

'Don't worry. Erabus is on his way. I will be back in about half an hour. Check the back,' says Aeron.

She goes behind the house and disappears.

✳ ✳ ✳

In the back of the matatu, Cephas finds used books and a box of spray cans. He picks out a 'Laughing Yellow' and looks at the white walls across the way.

The sun is shining. The wind is dead.

He approaches the white walls and finds puddles of rainwater sitting at the foot of them. He stands over one and sees the world entire. One cumulus muscling into another; an occurrence of Nairoberry at the Machakos Bus Station, the thief pinballing from Blueband to Airtel to Coca-Cola; someone smoking a cigar getting out of a window on the 16th floor of Co-operative House and shoes come off dangling legs and freefall.

He is not sure what he wants to say on the walls. Usually, he looks at a letter or word and copies it. So he looks for a stray bit of newspaper or a milk or Omo packet the wind may have blown in. He finds nothing. In downtown he just looks up.

He aims at a white wall and sprays a yellow curl. But this is not what he wants.

He jumps and catches a window ledge. Balances over a puddle. Hooks a leg on a brick jutting out and presses down, a hand grasps the roof edge and he climbs on top. He sees another Kenyan monsoon cloudwall on the horizon. Dark and grey. But no wind yet. He looks down between gaps in the houses, hoping to find a discarded Tetrapak. He finds nothing. He jumps over to the next roof, finds another jutting brick and hangs over another window ledge. And he sees Aeron in a puddle.

She is seated on a chair. He figures out the angle and realizes she's in his house.

Then there is the sound of sliding feet. Erabus appears in the puddle. He is back. And at least he has the book in his hands. Cephas aims and sprays 'Human Evolution' on the wall. Yellow curls for the 'o's and 'u's and yellow slants for the 'v' and yellow lines for the rest. Erabus disappears behind the house.

Aeron takes off her bikini. The 'Laughing Yellow' goes click, click.

Aeron's sagging breasts rest on her stomach, which is coming out like a small potbelly. Erabus removes his pants but can't seem to get out of his underwear. He moves toward the door.

Cephas waits for a word.

Aeron puts a hand on top of her head and pulls her hair. It comes off and drags along the attached skin and reveals another body underneath. She throws the skin at the escaping Erabus who catches it and ends up holding Aeron's sagging breasts. Aeron has become the Coca-Cola girl. The one Erabus said had the curves every grown man wants to see. And Cephas sees two Coca-Cola girls in the puddle, one at the edge of downtown and another in his house. He sprays 'Coca-Cola' and runs out of wall space.

Another jutting brick. Another wall. Another puddle. A different angle of reflection.

Cephas sees himself in the puddle. He sprays a yellow curl out of inertia. He finds cracks in between bricks and puts his shoes inside them and positions himself in ways that defy gravity. He can see the white wall in the puddle.

Aeron has words and letters tattooed all over her. Cephas can't see them all because Erabus is stroking his hand over the Coca-Cola's body. It's certainly not Aeron any more. Aeron is on the floor, all folded over. Erabus is cupping the breasts and Cephas knows this because the shape looks like the curve of the skyscrapers around Johnny Walker. He looks into the puddle to double check. The words on Coca-Cola are like words on a map. Cephas lets his right hand swing like a pendulum and sprays yellow doodles: '**Nairobi – Escarpment – Naivasha**'.

Cephas is upside down sometimes, somersaulting other times. In the puddle he thinks it looks like he is flying like a bird but he has never seen one. He swings a bit too much and his knee knocks on the old bench. He looks into the puddle and sees Erabus has been bowled out in between his legs and only one gently curving stump is all that remains. Cephas doesn't understand why they didn't invite him to join in their cricket game.

Coca-Cola goes on the bed and puts her knees up and spreads them. There is glitter on her body and the whole shape of her looks exactly like lights on buildings downtown.

More words. '**Out of Kenya**', '**John 1:5**', '**Out of Africa**', '**Light**', '**Darkness**.'

Then Erabus moves over her and something locks inside Cephas.

Then the puddles dwindle and evaporate and Cephas' fingers are stained yellow.

He gets down and goes to the matatu. After a while Erabus and Coca-Cola come and join him. A cool wind finally blows. It's four o'clock in the afternoon.

So Aeron was always Coca-Cola. And she is now wearing Aeron's bikini and she does not have sagging breasts. And she smells of white-collar perfume.

'Are you Aeron?'

Coca-Cola smiles and Cephas thinks he can taste spearmint in the smile.

'You don't mind if I can still call you Aeron?'

'No problem.'

They all sit in the front. Erabus hands over the **Human Evolution** book to Cephas. The ice-cream wind of the Kenyan monsoon blows in through the matatu windows and Aeron closes all of them.

The matatu roars. Aeron is smoking a cigarette and the ash is falling on her bikini straps. Music booms. They cut through the downtown and city easily, the matatu cares for nobody on the road. It's the bully and it's the beast. They go past Blue Band and Coca-Cola, past Airtel and Johnny Walker. Past Tusker. Cephas likes to think they are leaving downtown behind forever. They move onto the highway which will take them to the escarpment.

It becomes a long road and there is the shining glass of skyscrapers on both sides. Cephas sees uniformed guards with alsatians, who have their tongues sticking out, at the entrance of every skyscraper. Sometimes he sees a Kenya

Army tank. And then domes. Cephas can read out three big signs: '**Nuclear Power Station**', '**Karen Naivasha Grid Sect 3.4**', '**Karen Nakuru Grid Sect 3.9**'. He then sees a boy wearing torn clothes roaming the skyscraper pavements. He wonders if he is another spider.

Cephas flips through the pages of *Human Evolution*. First he sees a point on a map written in big bold letters. 'NAIROBI'. Then on the next page there is a gorilla-like creature sitting on what Erabus once told him was grass. He turns the pages and sees the gorilla becoming upright and on the last pages he is standing straight and looks like Erabus. Muscles and hair on his chest. There are some things next to the sky in the photo.

'Hey bro. What are these?'

Erabus looks sad and empty. Like he never found something which he always thought was there. Cephas finds a button and turns down the booming music and pokes Erabus in the ribs.

'What are these?'

'Those are birds,' says Erabus.

They look like the small 'v's he has sometimes drawn. There is a half-human, half-gorilla picture under them. Bold letters on the next page: '**Homo Erectus**'. He has sprayed that word before. He turns to another page and it almost comes off. He sees a map and he sees more bold letters: '**Homo Sapiens Trajectory Out of Africa**'. And he sees on the map points written in bold letters. '**Elmentaita**', '**Naivasha**', '**Nakuru**', '**Turkana**', '**Ethiopia**', '**Europe**'. They are following this route, he is sure.

An early evening falls on the world. The sun is setting, the skyscrapers now look orange, and the sky goes dark.

He opens the pages in the middle of the book. This is the photo he remembered from morning. It's a valley and there are lakes and mountains and great plains of grass on it. This is what Erabus promised him they would see.

'Have you really seen it for yourself?'

Erabus does not answer. Cephas sees confusion in him. He

sees him looking at the buildings left and right, as if it is all unfamiliar or like they are not supposed to be there.

'Aeron, are we going the right way?' asks Erabus.

'Yes,' replies Aeron, pinching Erabus' cheeks.

Then, just like that, Cephas wants to feel the ice-cream wind of the Kenyan monsoon and he opens his window. And, just like that, they arrive at the escarpment and the world entire opens up under them but Cephas has no time to look because the wind ruffles the pages of **Human Evolution** and sends them flying out the window.

'No! What are you doing?' Aeron shouts, and leans over and manages to grab one page.

The other pages fly over the world entire which is the Rift Valley and Cephas finally sees it. There are no lakes or cratered volcanoes like Erabus had promised. The whole of the Rift Valley is lit up with fireflies. The pages of **Human Evolution** fly away like birds over a carpet of bulbs and neon. And there is a cloud of newspapers in the sky, luminous with a backlight.

Aeron stops the matatu in the middle of the road. She gets off and runs to the edge of the escarpment and puts her hands out wide. With the backdrop of the lit Rift Valley, she looks like the Jesus in Brazil that Cephas has seen in Ladybird books. Cephas and Erabus get off the matatu and join Aeron at the edge of the escarpment. It starts raining but the three of them just keep looking down and get soaked and don't care.

The fireflies curve over what should have been mountains and dip back into the valley and rise up again over another mountain. Again it looks like Coca-Cola lying on her back and downtown lit up at night. The wind makes the lights shimmer and the locked thing inside Cephas unlocks. In the shimmering he thinks he sees a giant Erabus going over a giant Coca-Cola. There are cricket stadiums lit up down there and it seems the outfield must be very large. There are airplanes landing into the fireflies. Dambooze is shitting in a toilet in the Rift Valley.

It stops raining and there are puddles all over the ground and road, reflecting the neon and bulbs of the Rift Valley. Erabus sits down on a rock and looks into one of the puddles and Cephas sees him.

'Well, it doesn't matter. Let's keep pushing on,' says Aeron.

As Aeron walks back to the matatu, Cephas gets a look at the wet page she grabbed earlier. It's a photo of a lady who looks as Coca-Cola as her. There are big bold letters under it: **'Homo Sapiens'**.

The matatu roars. Cephas walks up to his brother and catches him on the arm. Erabus gets up from the stone and the two of them walk away from the puddle.

The blue matatu moves and the shadow of two heads cuts the emblazoned slogan on the blue body – **'There is Light in the Darkness, But the Darkness Does Not Understand It'** – into a shape. The matatu moves and now there is an empty road with the very same shadow of two heads cast on it.

Then the lights go out of the world. There is a blackout. The Rift Valley disappears together with the cloud of newspapers. The moon peeps out from behind a mountain and shines on Lake Elmentaita. The crater of Mount Longonot is the open mouth of Rift Valley and it is speaking to them with the voice of the wind. An airplane has lost control and is dropping out of the sky. There are stars in the sky and stars in Lake Elmentaita. Cephas looks at the brightest one. The light goes deep into his iris and he sees planets orbiting the star.

Mehul Gohil is a writer born and living in Nairobi, Kenya. He won the 2010 'Kenya I Live In' short story competition organized by Kwani Trust. His stories have been published in *Kwani? 6*. He is a Don DeLillo and Michael Jackson fanatic.

Mama's Walk

Grace Khunou

THERE WAS AN UNLIKEABLE QUIETNESS in how Mama went about her life. She did not complain, fight, celebrate or get involved. There was a certain absence in her presence. Her eyes were distant. She would stare into space instead of cry or shout. She automatically took care of the chores without asking much of my brothers and me and she had fewer and fewer answers to my endless whys and whats. She would instead look at me, shake her head and go about whatever she was doing. She confused me. I wondered what happened to her. When I was a baby, she giggled a lot and her cheeks turned red like ripe nectarines.

Now, she did not smile, play with us or get involved with the other mothers. She did not belong to a *stokvel* or play Mochina like MmaPalesa and Gogo, from across the street. All her time was spent staring at the walls, scrubbing the floors, and washing our old torn clothes. Our house was small, tidy and cold. Because Mama was there but never there, my younger brothers and I stayed away from home as much as possible, and she did not seem to mind.

Mama was strange; on top of all her weirdness she went ahead and chose a man like Pitso, my father, for a husband. He was unlike the other fathers. My friend Palesa's father brought home the wages at the end of the week. On Friday afternoons she did not play till her mother called her like she did on most days. She rushed home before dark, before her father arrived with the big red and white Kentucky Fried Chicken box and the black plastic bags with the 'hotstuff'.

Palesa's house was a buzz of excitement and merriment on Friday evenings, MmaPalesa's soft giggles turned into hearty laughter, and the sway of her hips became more animated as she moved from the effects of the hotstuff and mama Miriam Makeba's 'Phata Phata'. She was alive and generous, she was always happy to have us around. Palesa was very lucky to have her as a mother.

Since there was nothing to rush home for, we stayed at Palesa's house until after the serving of the fried chicken. Once we had filled our tummies, we then reluctantly went home. Friday nights were like a recurring nightmare at our house. Papa did not come home in a rush like all the other fathers, there was no swaying of Mama's hips, suggestive giggles and dancing to mama Miriam Makeba's melodies. There was instead a loud, empty silence, empty pots, and a stifling order, with everything properly folded and in its place. Papa never came back with plastic bags in his hands and big buckets of chicken for my brothers and me, and Mama seemed unaware and unable to do anything about it.

Papa, like the other men who worked in Daveland, the factory area behind Baragwanath Hospital, knocked off at two pm on Friday afternoons, but he mysteriously arrived in the early hours of Saturday morning, all the wages gone. We could all hear his singing and toyi toying from the beginning of the block: 'Girilagijima, gijima, hai, hai…' he sang and danced all the way to our house – like a madman. By the time he got to our gate, he was already yelling: 'Wake up, wake up, comrades, or have you forgotten who you are, you are named after heroes, big men; soldiers, come greet your father,' he screamed at my brothers as he struggled to unlock the door and then he would topple into the house like he had been pushed in by some large animal, leaving the kitchen door wide open.

Slovo and Castro, my younger brothers, would sleepily get out of their blankets in obedience to their father like real soldiers. They would stand there waiting for further instruction in their three-quarter-torn pyjamas. 'Come close, why are you standing there like you are silly little girls?' He screamed when the boys did not move close to greet him – like a rehearsed movie, the sequence began with the usual lecture: 'What kinds of comrades are you? Are you not soldiers? You must learn how to take instructions, my boys! You must listen to your commander! Stand up! Come on, wake up.' He would shout them out of their slumber. 'Are you like your father or are you mama's boys? What kind of men will you be if you are always listening to your mother, you will never grow up to be strong like me – wake up, this is the jungle!'

Mama remained buried in her pillow, her body stiff like a log on the ground. Did she die when she went to sleep? How could she not hear Papa's shouting and Slovo and Castro's sobs? Did she not care? Was she quietly praying for the inevitable not to happen? Was she in deep sleep where her being was transported to the beyond, somewhere fun where she laughed, giggled and swayed her hips? I wondered when she would stand up for my brothers and tell Papa a word or two. My hopes were always dashed when, as usual, my turn to perform in Papa's nightmare came. 'Come on, Koko, wake up and give your father his food,' he would irritably shout. 'Or are you like your mother – stubborn and useless?'

He knew there was no food. Where would the food come from? I thought, with a hot temper rising from my gut. He knew there was no food; he was just playing a silly game, a game to get to my mother, to get her up, to get her to do something, maybe to shout and scream. Like me, Papa seemed disappointed at her refusal to respond. Then I got the courage to say, 'but papa there is no food'. Before I could say anything else, the hot temper I felt earlier bottled up in my chest, and I began to sob uncontrollably. At my response and tears, Papa reacted by throwing his shoes on the elevated bed propped up at the corner of our one-roomed *mkhukhu*. As the shoes hit Mama, she for the first time since the beginning of the nightmare stirred and sat up with an apologetic look

on her face and said something inaudible as usual and that
infuriated my father even more. He started hurling insults at
her: 'Lazy witch, you think I do not know about the *muthi*?
Cleaning the house like you are godly, sitting here like you are
better than everyone else – I know about the *sangoma* that
you visit when you go to your mother's house. You want to
kill me and my children – *o moloi* man.' The insults turned to
a physical tussle when Papa jumped up and pulled Mama out
of bed and started beating her, not caring that we were there
witnessing all of it; unmoved by our loud cries and Mama's
screams for him to stop. She never struggled or tried to fight
him back.

On witnessing Mama's submission to Papa's insults and
punches, I got angry, and I stopped crying and just sat there
watching and thinking: why does she allow him to do all these
things and say all these lies about her? I wanted to shake her
awake, and shout into her face and let her know that she could
take him on and win. Why didn't she do something, hit back,
find a job, buy a house and take my brothers and me away?
Why, when she was stronger and more sober than Papa, did
she allow him to do this to her, to us?' She could easily get
help. But no, she kept on being the silent wife and mother.
She refused to let her voice be heard. She did not shout or
ask for help from *bomalome* or *boragwane*. She did not go to
the maintenance court on 15 Market Street like MmaMalome
Sarah did when Malome refused to bring home the wages.
She didn't do anything.

I refused to participate in the charade. I stalled every time
she asked me to do some chore that would benefit Papa. I
would remove pieces of meat from his plate. Why did he have
to get more meat than all of us? I rinsed instead of properly
washing his smelly socks, and pretended not to hear when
he called me to do something for him. On the odd days when
there was money in his pockets, I would help myself to a few
coins without being seen. I sang loudly on Sunday mornings
when he was sleeping. I rebelled and refused to be made into

a proper girl, into my mother. I could not behave like things were normal when they were not.

*** *** ***

During one of my complaints about the depressing mood and our situation to Palesa, MmaPalesa overheard and came to the stoep where we were sitting. She sat down with us and warmly stuck her nose into our business: '*Ao moratuwa gotlaloka neh* things will get better *oautlwa*.' MmaPalesa and Mama had walked the same path in their early life. They worked at the same factory for their first job in Booysen's and they married at the same time. When they were young mothers and wives they used to meet at the same stokvel where they saved money. Those were the good times, MmaPalesa remarked. 'Pale, do you remember MmaKoko took care of you when I was a stay-in at my first job in the kitchens?' '*Ao*,' Palesa responded. This was news to me, as well as to her. I had no idea my mother had taken care of Palesa when she was younger.

Very early on the morning of Easter Saturday, MmaPalesa walked through our gate. I got worried. What could be the matter now? Did something happen to Palesa? None of the adults in our street had been to our house in many years. I ran towards her and felt relieved when she returned my greeting with a smile, and warmly enquired, 'Is Mama home, Moratuwa?' MmaPalesa wore the right clothes, walked the right way, smelled sweet like the flowers Gogo kept in her neat, colourful garden and the sound of her voice was hypnotic. As I woke from that moment's daydream, I remembered that I had not responded to her question and embarrassingly answered with an uncharacteristically low, '*Ea Mme Mama o teng*'.

Mama responded shyly to the knock on our door, like she did not want MmaPalesa there, but she hid her displeasure and asked her guest to sit down. Thank god she did not act out her disapproval at MmaPalesa's visit; she had brought us good news. As I sat in the background eavesdropping on their conversation, I felt my heart pump a little faster and my head spin a little with happiness when she announced that one of her madam's friends, MmaViljoen, needed someone to come work for her and she thought Mama would be the best candidate. On hearing the news, Mama shifted in her seat and smiled a little. She said: '*Kea leboga* – I will be ready on Tuesday morning to go with you to Roodepoort for the job.'

When MmaPalesa left, Mama got up with a lot of determination in her voice and instructed us to put on our shoes for a visit to our grandmother's house in Orlando. Although people used taxis from Diepkloof to Orlando, we could not afford that luxury, we had to walk. It was a long walk and Slovo kept asking me to carry him, which I could not do since I was also already burdened by my grumbling tummy, the unco-operative sun and my heavy, tired feet. Castro was happily sleeping on Mama's back, ignorant of our troubles. As we walked to Orlando, Mama started talking to me about the chores I would have to do from Tuesday; she was gentle and kind in how she gave the instructions. She held my hand and squeezed it as she assured me that things would get better when she started working.

It was good to see Grandma after so long. Mama started crying when we walked in the gate, and Grandma cried with her as she walked her into the house. I was not sure why they cried, it was supposed to be a good day. Mama had just been offered a job. I was unable to eavesdrop on their conversation; Grandma did not like children who hung around when adults were talking, so when she gave me that look I went outside to play with my brothers and cousins. We stayed at Grandma's house the whole day and enjoyed a good meal of fried fish, rice and beetroot, which we downed with coke. We left Grandma's house with full stomachs and smiles on our faces. Grandma opened her purse and gave Mama a few notes as we got ready for our taxi ride back home. The money was to allow her to go to her new job on Tuesday.

When Mama started working, I was excited that she would start to bring all sorts of nice things home like MmaPalesa did for Palesa and her brothers and sisters, but I was shocked at how much responsibility I had to take on. I was not used to so many chores; Mama never taught me much or expected much from me. I had to wake up an hour earlier than I was used to so as to get the boys up ready. Prepare soft porridge, fold and tidy up our blankets. Slovo went to the same primary school as me, and Castro had to be dropped off at crèche on the way. After school I had cleaning to do, which took up all my playing time. After a few weeks I had a system going; I knew where and how to cut corners. When Mama got off the bus, I got an alert from my playmates. Then I would run home. Once all the work was done I ran to the gate in anticipation, not wanting to miss the magic of her walk home.

I always enjoyed watching Mama walk home after her long days at the kitchens. Since she took the job offered by MmaPalesa at Easter, life had improved for us. We ate better, had better clothes and school shoes. Sometimes she made money available for the school lunch *kota*, my favourite – quarter bread with mashed potatoes, minced meat and *atchar*. However, other things remained unchanged. Papa still sang and woke Castro and Slovo when he got home in the early hours of the morning, and still refused to bring the wages home on payday. He did not hit Mama any more but the shouting and insults increased with every passing weekend.

I also started seeing Mama as less weird. Although she still did not mix with the other mothers or fight or scream at Papa when he did the same, she had changed. I felt a little closer to her. After our intimate talk when we walked to Orlando on Easter Saturday, she spoke to me more often, complimenting me on the work I did around the house and saying how well I was taking care of Slovo and Castro.

'You are quite the little Mrs over here – you have completely taken over, o *godileneh!* Thank you Koko,' she would say with a reassuring smile. She shared stories from her bus and those about MmaViljoen's funny neighbours. She dressed better: even though most of her new clothes were MmaViljoen's *ou klere*, she looked impressive. Although there was a closeness building between us, there was something mysterious about her: a slipperiness I struggled to pin down.

The growing attachment between us was enhanced by the magic I felt when I watched Mama walk home from work. I felt something like a deep, unexplainable connection. She walked slowly, like she was in deep thought, and at the same time like she was happy to be on her way. Her steps seemed contemplated, like a dance to a slow, rhythmic song. The sway of her hips brought admiring looks from the men and women walking past. The last light of the day that accompanied the walk made her silhouette look magical, like she was unreal. I wanted to possess her, to be her. What was she thinking? I wondered. Was she happy the work day was over? Was she weary to come back to her one-roomed *mkhukhu*, with three children and an angry husband, without the typical comforts that most of her friends had? I did not know. I could only secretly wonder what was going on in her mind.

She walked like she was breathing her last, like she would drop dead and die there and then and never have the opportunity to do it again. But there was a beauty in that end-of-day walk home; it was not hurried, or filled with much concern. Dust was not kicked up by her slow-moving legs, making the road seem tarred. The usual loudness of the township at knock-off time was magically muted to my ears, as the mixed smells of paraffin, smoke from Umbaula's and MmaButhelezi's burning pap were dulled to my senses. I could only feel my heart pounding with anticipation. My mother was on her way home.

Her walk home always brought us some goodies, *mgena ndlini* – a parcel of sweets, fruits or leftovers from her lunch to say sorry she had gone so long from us. Was the slow walk a moment to collect herself? To bring herself to accept that her life had changed but not quite in ways that she wanted?

Her slow movements intrigued and disturbed me at the same time.

∗ ∗ ∗

One day, four months after Mama started working for MmaViljoen, I was surprised when our game of Umgusha ended and we all went home before my usual warning that Mama was getting off her bus. I got home, did the finishing touches to my chores, and the waiting began. By the time I checked, it was dark and late and Mama was still not on her way. I waited and cried myself to sleep for three days.

In Mama's absence, Papa became the father we never had. He was out with friends less often and brought goodies on Friday afternoons. He had funny answers to my whys and whats and taught Castro and Slovo some complex soccer moves. He even cooked Sunday lunch with ease, as if he had done it many times. Our house was not neat and tidy like before, but it was warm like I always wanted. Often I stood at the gate until it was late and dark; my waiting did not bring her back. My mother's walk home, I realized, was beautiful because she was walking back to me: it was a love song, a gentle reminder that said I mattered.

Grace Khunou was born and raised in Diepkloof, Soweto. She is a sociologist and lecturer at the University of the Witwatersrand. Her first anthology of poems, *Cosmic Vibrations*, was published in 2011.

Moving Forward

Lauri Kubuitsile

I LIE IN BED AND LISTEN. I think Dad's gone – his shift starts at six and Ma's not yet awake. I get up quickly and put on my school uniform, grab my backpack and slip out into the cool morning. Today I don't feel like seeing them.

It's still early, just past six, so I wander around, killing time. I find myself heading towards Phenyo's house. I woke up thinking about her. I have an urge to see her today. While I'm walking, I think about when we were kids. We used to like to play down by the Lotsane River. There's a special place we had where a group of four flat boulders lined up in a row, hidden under a canopy of morula trees. When we were small we used to pretend it was a train. We'd take turns driving the boulders away, away to places that made us happy.

Phenyo always chose the jungle or the Arctic Circle or China. Faraway, exotic places. 'Drive me to Saturn, Boni!' she'd say, and while I was driving she'd point out landmarks. The purple oceans, the flying teddy bears, the trees made of ice cream. Her world was always big. Too big for Palapye, for Botswana. I used to be afraid it was too big for me.

Mine was always small, simple and familiar. 'Take me to Gaborone. Drive me to Joburg.' I didn't have any ice-cream trees. No teddy bears would be found when we arrived. I was just happy to be on the way with her. She'd always say: 'One day, Boni, I'll get us out of this place. You wait and see. We're going to go somewhere, you and me.'

I stand in front of her mother's two and a half. It's early but I can hear the baby crying. I wait for a moment and wonder if today might be the right day to knock on her door. Her mother doesn't like me. Last time I was there she shouted I was coming round hoping to get Phenyo pregnant again. I felt bad about that most because I saw Phenyo's face. Those words hurt her. Her mother's such a bitch, always has been, worse since the baby and all. I didn't trouble to sort her out, let her know I wasn't like that. MmagoPhenyo's not big on listening. I decide to give it a miss and head for the bus rank.

'Whatzup Littleman?' BraT says, when I come up to where he's set out his table.

'*Ga ke bue*, BraT.'

'So it's your big day, eh? A man now, 18 years old. *O batla go dirang?* You need to start making plans.' I'm a bit chuffed BraT remembered my birthday.

'Maybe I'll set up shop with you, BraT?' I tease.

'Ao! Littleman, you need to set your sights higher than that. Mmoloki used to say how his little brother was gonna be something one day.'

I nod but say nothing. I wonder about that, about the something Mmoloki thought I might be. BraT reaches in his bag and pulls out a small, black box. He pushes the box into my hand and looks away as if he's embarrassed. 'Here.'

'What's this?' I ask, looking down at the box.

'It's your birthday isn't it? Open it.'

I look at him but don't know what to say. BraT's been like that. It's like he thinks he needs to fill Mmoloki's shoes somehow. He's good that way and I want him to know that but can't find a way to say it without making us both feel stupid.

He looks at his watch and then up and down the bus rank. 'Wonder where Zero is,' he mutters, mostly to himself.

Nowadays, BraT and Zero work the bus rank with Find the Lady. BraT lays out three cards on an overturned cardboard box. One is the queen of hearts, the lady. The one the mark's meant to find. He flips the cards around back and forth and if the mark finds the lady then they double their money, which only happens until it doesn't. Zero acts as the back-up man just in case the mark is slow to put his money down. People are always hopeful they can get something from nothing so it's an easy way to take their money. They're just idiot fools, everyone knows the world isn't like that.

'You gonna open it or not?' BraT asks. 'I know you're gonna like it. It's something Mmoloki would have liked too.'

I like the way he speaks about my brother. I open the box and inside is an iPod, a new one. I'm touched that he thought to give me a birthday present at all, but even more touched that it was bought, not stolen. I turn it around in my hands.

'Thanks BraT. This is cool.'

'I already loaded a few songs.'

I look at him and he nods. Nothing else to say. I know what songs he's loaded for me, it's the CD BraT and Zero made with Mmoloki. They had a band: Zero on drums, BraT on keyboard, and Mmoloki on lead guitar and vocals. They played Afrojazz and pop, lots of original songs that either Mmoloki or BraT wrote. They were just starting out, but that's when everything changed.

Mmoloki knew it was coming. 'That old man's a fool if he thinks I'm going underground,' he'd told me more than once. 'This is my life. Only my life. I'm not wasting it down there.'

We were all sitting around the table that evening when Dad said, 'You start on Monday.'

We all watched him; Me, Mmoloki and Ma, letting our plates of *palache* and stew cool in front of us. I held my breath. It'd been building for months. Ever since Mmoloki failed his form five, Dad had been talking about getting him a job down at Morupule Coal Mine where he worked. Mmoloki hadn't said much, you didn't with our father. No one did, not even our mother. He spoke and we all listened. We pleaded our cases with Ma. She sometimes found a way to get around him, but mostly not. Mostly we just did what he told us to do to make things easier.

'I already have a job,' Mmoloki said, his hands hanging at his side. 'I made P500 last week in Gabs. I'm earning money.' Mmoloki spoke in a soft voice but I could hear the rage simmering underneath.

Dad pushed his plate away. 'Do you know what I had to do to get you that job? Do you? And then you want to sit here and be ungrateful?'

'I'm not ungrateful. I'm just not doing it.'

I sat as still and small as I could and waited.

Like he was reaching for the salt, Dad punched Mmoloki in the face. Blood spurted from his nose. Ma went for a towel but Dad stopped her: 'Sit!'

She sat back down.

The effort set his wonky lungs off and he started coughing. He reached for the water my mother handed him, not taking his eyes off my brother. His eyes as hard as rock.

Mmoloki stood up. Blood dripped on his T-shirt, making a red spot on his chest like his heart was bleeding through. He said nothing and walked out.

He was gone for most of that week, but then on the Thursday evening, after Dad drove off to the bar, Mmoloki reappeared. He must have been watching outside, waiting for the car to leave. He said he'd come to get his stuff.

'Go to your room, Bonolo,' Ma ordered me when he walked in the door.

I sat in the doorway of the room I shared with Mmoloki and listened.

'He's sick, Mmoloki. He didn't mean any of that. He didn't mean to hurt you,' Ma said. 'It's the stress and all.'

'Is it? Then why'd he punch me in the face? Why does he hit you? Don't lie to yourself, he means to hurt you just like he meant to hurt me.'

'But the job, Mmoloki. They're expecting you to show up on Monday.'

'They can expect me until hell fucking freezes because I won't be pitching up down at that mine any time soon.'

'But what about us? What about me and Bonolo?' Ma said.

'What do you mean? This has nothing to do with you.'

'It does. They're going to fire your father if he doesn't get better. How will we live? What will we do?'

I tried to hear the rest of the conversation, but they lowered their voices. I only heard Ma crying and then the door closing. At 18, he became a coal miner just like his father. The exact thing he swore he'd never do.

I put the earphones in and press play and there's Mmoloki, singing like I could reach out and touch him, his voice so strong and clear. I close my eyes and listen and think about how much I love him. How much I miss him. I decide not to close my heart off today and I let the good memories flow over me.

Even though I left early, I'm already late for school so I decide it's better to give it a miss. The teachers give me a lot of leeway nowadays. What was school anyway, just a way to pass the time. I was certain I wasn't passing my form five, so what's the point? I'm never going to go off to UB like the successful kids, so it doesn't matter if I'm there or not.

I head for the patch of trees behind the mall. It's the way Phenyo passes most days. I sit down on a broken brick and wait. It's been months since I've spoken to her. I miss her and I'm tired of the silence. Today I want to see her, I want her to see me.

We'd always been best friends, but then she met Tops who drove a combi and gave her money every day. For a while she didn't want anything to do with me. She only spent time with Tops. Once I tried to tell her he was no good for her, but she wouldn't listen. I knew he treated a lot of girls like that. He didn't care about her really, just like he didn't care about the other girls. I told her that, about the other girls, and she told me none of that mattered, that she knew what she was doing. Then she got pregnant and Tops disappeared. When she called him, he wouldn't pick up. Later, after the baby was born, he'd drop money at her house, money he skimmed off what he gave to the combi owner, but he didn't want anything to do with Phenyo. After that she stopped talking to me completely.

That was three months ago. Since then there's been this gap in my life, joining up with all of the other gaps. I'd see her around but she'd pretend she didn't see me. I'd pass by her house and try to get the courage to knock on the door and stop the quietness between us, but in the end I never did. Today, though, I want to see her. I want to talk to her.

I think about what BraT said, too. Eighteen ought to be a special day, a changing day. Ma should have made a fuss over me. Dad should have given me a talk about being a man now. But nothing. Since Mmoloki died they're like ghosts.

I look out over the mall where people set up tables to sell tomatoes and onions. The phone ladies open their yellow umbrellas and shopkeepers unlock burglar bars. The beginning of a new day.

Before, when Mmoloki was there, everything was different. He had something, a light or a kind of magnetic pull. You felt it. Everyone loved him, you just wanted to be around him. He had enough light for the both of us. I wasn't in the dark, it was easy to see things. But then it went out. And it's been like that ever since. Like living in a murky darkness. Ma and Dad and me, just feeling around, trying to stay in the corners and away from the edges, trying to keep from knocking into feelings too big to touch. And we've just been there, not moving, for so long. I was a kid, so I waited to follow, waited for someone to lead, but no one ever did. Well, I'm not a kid any more.

I look across and see Phenyo coming. I take the earphones off. She's in her school uniform, but late like usual. I stand up and walk to her.

'Hey, Phenyo,' I say, scared, not certain if she'll see me today, hoping so badly she will.

She looks up and for a moment I think she'll walk past me but then she doesn't.

'Where'd you get that?' she asks, pointing to the iPod.

'BraT gave me.'

'Stolen?'

'Nope. It's new. Look.' I hand her the iPod.

'Why'd he do that?'

I look down at the ground. 'It's my birthday,' I mumble to a passing plastic bag.

'Oh... right.' Then I can hear her remembering about Mmoloki. 'Oh... yeah.'

'Phenyo,' I start, 'I'm sorry about...' And then I'm not sure what to say since I'm not sure what I did to make her stop talking to me.

'No, no, Boni, it's me. I'm the one. I got all mixed up with everything. I let you down. I promised we'd go places, you and me, and instead I let Tops mess me around and now there's the baby and... well, I'm sorry,' she says. 'I was a fool to ever think I could do something else, be something I'm not.'

Then she's quiet for a while and I'm quiet too. I don't like that she thinks that way. It's not true. 'You can do anything, P, anything you want.'

She looks up at me, her face soft. 'That's my Boni.'

We're quiet for a while, trying to work our way back to normal. A combi passes and for a moment I think it's Tops, but it's not.

Phenyo ignores the passing combi and says, excited now, 'Hey man! You're 18! Legal and everything. We need to celebrate! Let's go and get some chicken, I'm starving. Tops gave me P100 last night to buy the baby formula. I say we make a party for the birthday boy.'

She smiles at me, that big crooked smile she gets when she's really happy, and holds out her hand. I take it and we walk up toward the junction. She's still beautiful. People at school like to say she's damaged goods because of the baby and all, but I don't think so. I think Phenyo's as beautiful now as she was the first time I saw her in standard one. I act like I don't want her to make a fuss about my birthday, but I actually do. I like that she's going to use Tops' money on me. I like it a lot.

We walk a bit and she asks: 'So how you feeling about this whole birthday thing then, Boni? Is it okay now?' She asks because she knows everything. I could always talk to Phenyo, I could tell her anything. It helped during that time.

Mmoloki had been at the mine for two months. Despite what he'd promised BraT, he never had time for the band. Any time off he spent getting drunk or stoned or sleeping. He never wanted to sing. Songs came from a place he couldn't find any more.

I was at school that day, my cake and presents waiting for me at home afterwards. It was my 16th birthday. Back then, school was good, I didn't need leeway. I was passing and teachers spoke about 'my bright future'. Mr Dithebe came into the Setswana lesson and Mma Rannoba looked at me and I knew.

I went out of the classroom and saw my Dad standing there in his work clothes, still covered in coal dust, and I knew it straight away. I knew Mmoloki was dead. I didn't need anything else. I didn't need to know that the wall of coal collapsed on him. I didn't need to know he screamed until he couldn't any more. That they weren't fast enough, that they didn't have the machine they needed, and that by the time they did it was too late. Suffocated by the coal, after two months of it choking the life out of him.

On the day Mmoloki died my father lost his air too. Like a balloon, he just deflated. Nothing was left in him. Even now. He barely talks. Where before he liked to control everyone, now he doesn't control anything.

Phenyo buys us both two pieces and chips. She's nice like that, generous and all. She smiles at me as we eat. I smile back. I used to dream about us getting married one day. I'd get a job and take care of her. We'd build a little house, maybe have kids. Where Phenyo wanted to travel the world, pulling me by the hand behind her, I wanted to stay still and quiet with her by my side.

'I wanted today to be my birthday, nothing more,' I say, when we're finished eating and just sitting. 'I'm tired of it being some sick celebration. That's all. I want to stop thinking about Mmoloki like that. He's dead. People die. People have to fucking get over it.'

I hear my voice rising and I can see alarm on Phenyo's face. 'No... sorry. It's just I've felt so heavy, so heavy I feel like I can't walk sometimes. The day comes and I feel like it's going to crush me. Do you get that, P? I think you get that, don't you?'

I need her to get it. I need someone to get it. Her, especially.

'Listen, Boni, you have the right to some happiness. Believe me, I so get it.'

She collects our rubbish and buys me an ice-cream cone for dessert. She takes a lick before handing it to me. 'For luck,' she says.

We head down to the river, to our boulder train. Seems the right place to be today. We climb up onto the large flat one at the front where the driver used to sit. It's cool from the shade of the trees. We lie back, quiet, sucking morulas and spitting out the pits, looking at the sky.

'You remember the boulder train, Boni?' she asks.

'Sure.'

She's quiet for a time. 'It was nice then. Like everything was possible.' I don't say anything but I know just what she means.

'So who's watching the baby?' I ask Phenyo after a while. I'm watching the cotton clouds drift, thinking about my happy full stomach. Thinking about how much just being there with Phenyo is making me feel better.

'My ma. She told me I'm a fool and I might as well leave the baby for her to take care of. I don't mind. The whole thing is so boring anyway.'

I can feel Phenyo's leg leaning against mine. I like it. I want to touch her thigh, but I think she might get angry. I watch the clouds and think about the fact that today is my birthday and Phenyo is next to me and how that's a very nice thing. When I woke up, I thought it would be a terrible day like always, but it's not. It's a good day.

I take the iPod out and I put one earphone in my ear and one in Phenyo's. I pick my favourite track. It's a song BraT wrote called 'Tsala ya Me'. Mmoloki's singing in his clear, pitch-perfect voice. He's singing about doing what's needed for your friend. The song is just right for that moment. We lie on the warm boulder looking up at the ocean blue sky with its sailboat clouds and I see Phenyo is crying silently.

I look at her and wonder what her tears are about. Is she crying because Tops doesn't care for her any more? Or for the baby she didn't want, or because her mother took the baby away and called her a fool? Was she crying about Mmoloki still singing in my iPod even though he's cold and dead in the ground? Or is she crying because the boulder train doesn't let her see ice-cream trees any more?

The song finishes and Phenyo closes her eyes. Her neck is wet from tears and I reach forward and wipe them away. Then she crawls into my arms and I hold her. And it feels nice, the first thing to feel nice for a very long time. I hold her and try not to think about what it all means. I hold her and think about my birthday and Mmoloki and what I'm going to do now that I'm 18. I hold her and wonder when the answers will come. And then I think that maybe they won't and I just need to keep moving forward. I hold Phenyo and wonder if moving forward feels something like this and I decide that I think maybe it does.

Lauri Kubuitsile is a full-time writer living in Botswana. She has numerous published books, primarily romance and books for children and young adults. She's married with two grown children.

Table Manners

BM Kunga

SHIRO SITS IN THE NURSERY, cradling her last-born in her arms. She runs her fingers slowly over her daughter's delicious little features. Her eyelids, fine as a butterfly's wings, remain closed, long dark eyelashes kissing the tip of a high cheekbone she inherited from her father. Her nose is undeniably her mother's – short, squat. It's a nose that staked a claim, put down roots and will not be moved. It straddles her face and owns it. Shiro loves it. It screams 'mine' every time she sees Nyambura and she considers it the strongest connection she has to her youngest. It gives her face some character – perfection is always boring. And without it, it would be impossible to appreciate just how delicate her mouth is, with its narrow lips and prominent Cupid's bow. Nyambura is an incredibly beautiful baby and Shiro is struck by an almost overwhelming sense of pride: she made this thing.

She wriggles around on the armchair trying to find a comfortable position. It's been a while since she held her baby like this. She pulls her in close and buries her nose in her soft hair. She smells amazing – all baby powder and sweet dreams. Shiro picks up a pudgy little hand and kisses the fingertips – she feels cold. She wraps her blanket tighter around her and tucks her hands securely inside.

Wairimu bursts into the nursery interrupting their time alone. Shiro stands up quickly and turns her back to the door, blocking out the light that is streaming in from the corridor. 'Shut the door, Wairimu,' she orders.

Wairimu does as she is told and whispers: 'Mr Chege sent me to get you. He said you've been a while and your lunch is getting cold. I can take the baby...'

'No,' Shiro spits and hugs Nyambura tighter to her chest. She continues, a little softer this time: 'She's quiet now, I'll put her down myself. Go reheat my plate, I'll be down in a minute.' Wairimu dawdles, picking toys off the floor. 'Wairimu, get the fuck out,' she hisses. Wairimu, shocked, shuts the door quietly behind her. Shiro is surprised at her anger. She hates swearing, thinks it's vulgar and cheap. 'I can put you to bed, love, can't I?' she sings to Nyambura. 'You're a good girl, quiet for mummy, aren't you?' She kisses her daughter, puts her down gently in her crib, tucking an extra blanket around her. She turns on the baby monitor and tiptoes out of the nursery, downstairs to lunch.

✳ ✳ ✳

'Finally. Praise the Lord.' Chege is in a fighting mood.

'Chege, please...' she begins, but is silenced by her mother sitting across the table from her, digging the heel of her shoe into her foot.

'Chege, please what? The food is cold,' he leans back in his chair scowling at her. She looks around the table. His plate is empty, so is her mother's. She hadn't asked them to wait and they obviously didn't. The only food that got cold was hers.

'I'm sorry Chege, but you know how it's been with Nya.' An uncomfortable silence settles in the room.

Her mother clears her throat. 'You know, Shiro, she'll get used to you. You just need to spend more time with her.'

'More time?' Chege explodes. 'She's here all day every day, doesn't do shit. What more time? You haven't touched that kid in months, that's why she's screaming. In three hours this house will be full of people and you're taking forever to quiet her down. Now that you've succeeded, tell me, what was so hard?'

Shiro looks at her hands knotted in her lap.

Wairimu walks into the dining room, a steaming plate of rice and *njahi* in one hand, a fistful of cutlery in the other. She sets the plate down in front of Shiro and proceeds to build a fortress of hardware around it. I can do this, Shiro thinks to herself and steals a glance at Chege, who is watching her keenly. Work from the outside in, she tells herself. There is no soup, so the spoons are automatically out. She picks each piece up, one by one, tests its weight in her hand. Chege begins to tap his fingers on his water glass. She is wasting his time. 'Shiro, for God's sake, think! What are you eating?'

'Rice and beans, Chege,' she responds.

'Christ,' he swears softly. 'The main course,' he stresses, 'is eaten with the fork and knife closest to the plate. He raises his eyebrows at her expectantly. She picks up the right cutlery and realizes that the only way she will be getting out of this one, is by finishing every last bite of food on her plate. She takes her knife and heaps a huge pile of rice onto her fork. Bending low, as close to her plate as possible, she shovels the dry, bland lump into her mouth. She sits back, proud that she didn't spill anything, but, as she chews, she notices the napkin, wedged between two glasses on her right. Napkin first. She should have remembered. She slides it out and pretends to dab at her mouth. While her mouth is covered, she uses her tongue to dislodge errant grains of rice stuck between her upper lip and her gums. She chews faster, open mouthed and swallows hard. She lowers the napkin, spreads it out on her lap and only then can she raise her eyes to meet her husband's. The look on his face is of pure disgust. 'Tell Wairimu to send Njambi and Junior into the living room – there are a couple of things we need to sort out before the guests arrive.' He walks out of the dining room and, after a little while, Shiro picks up her soup spoon and begins to eat.

'Look at you,' her mother starts.

'What?' Shiro shrugs, as she pours herself a glass of water.

'You don't even try.'

'Try what, ma? To eat with a fork and knife? I'm at home, my home.'

'But you could learn...'

'Really? Learn? This from a woman who eats with her hands when he's not watching?'

Her mother recoils from the statement. Chege frowns upon behaviour that he categorizes as 'intrinsic village Kenyan' and he is still within earshot.

'I try, Shiro. I try, he knows it and he respects it,' she states proudly. 'You'll eat later, your husband is waiting for us in the living room.' She storms out after Chege, leaving Shiro and her fast-diminishing appetite to follow in her wake.

❊ ❊ ❊

Chege is polishing the wooden icon that sits above the fireplace. He picked it up on a trip to Zanzibar, spent a fortune on the hideous little thing. Shiro has always hated it. The *mganga* who sold it to him told him it was carved out of the heart of the only tree to survive a huge fire that raged on the island centuries ago. It would bring him great luck. Although he isn't superstitious, he doesn't let the children touch it and tells the story to anyone who will listen.

Shiro sits down next to her mother as the maid rolls in a trolley with coffee and biscuits. Wairimu pulls a stool up in front of Chege. He whispers to her and Wairimu giggles. She sets his coffee cup down and stirs in two teaspoons of sugar. Chege mumbles again and she grabs her shirt and covers her cleavage with her hand. She maintains this awkward position until she's arranged his biscuits on a plate. She rolls the trolley over to Shiro and her mother.

'Thanks, Wairimu, we'll serve ourselves,' Shiro says.

'Thanks, Nimo,' he purrs, and she flees the room.

'Nimo.' That's how it always begins with him. At least that's how it was with their previous maid, Wambui – 'Bui' to Chege. Then, whispers and giggles. Wairimu is almost 40: it's part of the reason she was hired. Unless Chege does it simply to spite Shiro. She'll have to consider a houseboy – but that might not be wise, with a six-year-old girl in the house.

Njambi and Junior crash into the room and fling themselves onto their father.

'Daddy, I made a picture for teacher today,' Njambi says proudly.

'Daddy, me I coloured elephants.'

He peels them off and, still smiling, asks Junior to report what he'd done that day. Happy to be singled out, Junior repeats, 'Me I coloured elephants.' Chege turns him around and swats him twice on his bottom.

'We don't say "Me, I",' he shouts. 'I coloured pictures of elephants.' Junior, only five, knows that tears will get him the belt.

'I coloured pictures of elephants,' the little boy squeezes out. Njambi has already backed away out of reach and is pressed up against the living-room door.

'Sit down,' he commands. The two children take the sofa closest to the door. Shiro watches as her babies practise introducing themselves to imaginary guests, Njambi curtseying low and Junior balancing the tray of biscuits in his tiny hands. Chege is no doubt engineering an adorable family moment to show off to his boss and is determined that they execute it perfectly. He corrects their posture and makes them circle the room several times. Every time they walk in front of Shiro, she offers a tiny smile of encouragement. Neither one of them smiles back at her. When he is satisfied, he dismisses them and they tear out of the room.

'Quietly, or you'll wake the baby,' he screams, as they thunder up the stairs. Shiro snorts into her coffee and Chege turns on her. 'You spend the whole day with those two and they can't speak English. The other one, crying all the time. God, you're useless. What do you do around here?'

'Nya is quiet now,' Shiro says. 'I'll go check on her.'

'Don't go setting her off again,' he calls out after her. 'I don't want her howling when Mr Nderitu arrives.'

She walks up to the door of the nursery and presses her ear up against it. Her hand is shaking when she opens the door just a crack to pull the key from the inside. She shuts the door and locks it, drops the key into her shirt pocket. Now she's a little dizzy, so she sits at the top of the stairs, head between her knees until it passes. She takes the key from her pocket, stares at its lines and grooves. 'I am a good mother,' she declares out loud. With her free hand she wipes away the sweat that's pouring down her neck. She puts the key back in her pocket and goes to dress her children up for Chege's dinner party.

***

It's an hour to the party and Shiro finally has a moment to herself. She pours a few drops of vanilla-scented oil into her bath water and sinks a little lower in the tub so the water covers her ears. She closes her eyes and tries to figure out when it all had gone to hell.

They had just moved into their new house in Naivasha and Shiro was having trouble adjusting to her new life as a stay-at-home mom. She missed Nairobi, her friends, her old job. Njambi and Junior were growing up so fast and she felt as though she was missing their childhood. When Chege suggested they have another baby, she was surprised. He had thrown himself so completely into his new job that they barely spoke. They hadn't made love in months and now he wanted to make a baby?

'You need something to keep you busy.'

'I could take classes or something.'

'What for? You're sitting on an MBA, you want to waste more of my money?'

Shiro didn't know what to say. Chege knew she had tried

to find a job. It hurt her that he would throw that in her face. 'No baby, please Chege.' She wasn't interested.

'I'm tired of telling my workmates and the guys down at the club that my wife is unemployed and idle at home. Barefoot and pregnant, I can explain, but right now I look stupid. Like I picked you straight from the village.'

Chege had come up from nowhere, worked his way to the top and was systematically erasing every trace of the man he had once been. Image was everything. He had eased into their new life effortlessly, picking up the mannerisms and affected speech he believed went with his new status. Shiro struggled with the feeling that it was fraudulent – this mould he thought they had to squeeze themselves into, wasn't them. It never would be.

Her pregnancy was uneventful. Chege would parade her around the club, inviting his friends' wives to rub her belly and soliciting advice from them on how to raise children. Shiro had by that time moved into their guest wing, the baby the price she felt she had to pay for her food and board.

Nyambura was hard work from the day she was born. She never slept through the night, she refused to breastfeed and many nights Shiro would pour milk she had expressed from rock-hard breasts down the sink in the bathroom. Then there was the crying. She cried if Shiro picked her up, cried if she tried to feed her, sometimes cried if Shiro looked at her. Shiro was totally overwhelmed. She couldn't handle it. When Nyambura turned two months old, Shiro moved her mother into the house and the old woman took over.

Then Chege decided to throw this party. He desperately wanted to impress his boss, Mr Nderitu, and he considered it the perfect opportunity to teach his junior colleagues how a real man balanced a successful career and the demands of a young family. The entire week, he had been conducting rehearsals, deciding where everybody would sit, how they would be introduced to his workmates and running through the little anecdotes he was going to share. Shiro had to get her act together – perfect wife, perfect mother. He forced her to carry Nyambura around and practise the best poses to show her off. Not used to her mother, Nyambura went wild. She screamed and twisted and fought Shiro like she was possessed. Chege wouldn't let Shiro put her down.

'Shut that kid up – you're her mother,' he said.

Three days it continued, Chege yelling at her over Nyambura's wails. The house was a mess, deliveries of food and flowers coming in at all hours. There were strangers in her home, waxing the floors, polishing silver and knocking over expensive vases. She was pulled in a hundred different directions, to supervise floral arrangements, taste the canapés and select the perfect shade of green paint for the bathroom walls. She hadn't slept at all and still Chege wouldn't give in.

Just before lunch, on the day of the party, Chege had finally had enough.

'I don't think you understand how important this dinner is,' he said, as he laid his suit out on his bed. Shiro had Nyambura draped over her left shoulder like a towel. Nyambura was whimpering, hands balled up into angry little fists.

'I do, Chege. I don't know what to do with the baby. She just won't stop.'

'Well, you'd better figure it out or you'll have to go. Mr Nderitu is choosing a partner within the next two months. It's down to me and that arrogant fool, Mugambi. How can I run a company if I can't keep my family in line?'

'Go where?' she asked as she considered the options that they had. She hadn't spoken to anyone back home in ages. None of her friends had even met Nyambura. This was all she had.

'I don't care, but I can't have this mess in my house. Not today.'

She reached out to touch him and he pushed her hard into the wall. Nyambura began to cry again.

'Let Wairimu take the baby, please, Chege.'

He slapped her hard across the face. The first time he had

ever hit her. He walked downstairs to lunch and left Shiro and Nyambura crying in his bedroom.

Shiro rubbed her baby's back, 'Nya, please stop,' she pleaded. Nyambura only got louder. Shiro shuffled into the nursery and shut the door quietly behind her.

*** ***

She picks out a black dress from the back of her bedroom closet – an old favourite. It dips low in the front and hugs her curves, before falling in a long smooth line to the floor. She carefully applies her make-up, smooths down flyaway strands of hair with a bit of Vaseline. She tucks the key in her bra and dabs some perfume on her wrists. Wairimu walks into her room with Junior and Njambi, who have already had their dinner. Chege doesn't want them eating too fast or too much in front of the guests. 'I wanted to change Nya, but the door to the nursery is locked,' she says, staring straight at Shiro.

'I'll deal with Nya, but these two need to get downstairs. Go see if the chef needs any help.' She dismisses Wairimu casually, but her palms are sweating and it's taken a great deal of energy to keep her voice steady. She takes a child in each hand and goes to meet their guests.

Chege and Mr Nderitu are studying the wooden icon when she walks into the room. She watches Chege tell a story she's heard a million times before. Mr Nderitu picks up the icon and turns it over in his hands. He peers closely at the wooden base and she knows he's seen the tiny 'Made in China', carved into the bottom. He shows the icon to Chege, whose mouth falls open. Mr Nderitu's laughter rolls across the room and he calls over a junior partner to look. She watches Chege and sees the muscles in his temple working furiously, stretching the thin skin. He turns to one of the waiters who's working the room and mutters softly. The waiter takes the icon away and Chege steers Mr Nderitu in the direction of the bar.

Shiro takes a deep breath and crosses the room. 'Mr

Nderitu, *karibu sana,*' she begins, a huge smile plastered on her face.

'Thanks, Shiro. It's been ages. You've been missing in action at the club – why is Chege locking you up in the house?' he asks. Mr Nderitu has always been kind to her.

'She's so busy with Nyambura, she doesn't have time to get out. She's superwoman, this one,' Chege says and places a hand on her shoulder.

'She must be huge, how old is she now?'

Shiro stands perfectly still, her heart in her throat. Chege gives her shoulder a painful squeeze, then pulls Junior and Njambi away from her. 'She's almost eight months old. Time really flies, I mean look at these two.' Njambi curtseys quickly and Chege laughs. 'So cute, I don't know where she picked it up from.' Mr Nderitu seems impressed and engages the children in talk about school.

Chege pulls Shiro aside. 'Get a sweater. Your breasts are flapping all over the place.' Shiro excuses herself and leaves quietly.

On the way to her room, she pauses outside the nursery door. Maybe if they had stayed in Nairobi, or if Chege hadn't been so successful, or if she'd put in a little effort and tried to enjoy their new life some more, things might have turned out different.

By the time she gets back, the party has moved to the dining room. The maids are bringing out the first course. She takes her place at Chege's right and drapes her napkin across her lap. She looks around the table at all his friends. They seem to be having a good time. She waits until everybody has been served and picks up her spoon. Carrot and ginger soup. She asks Chege to pass her the basket of bread rolls. He beams at her. Mr Nderitu compliments her on her beautiful home and her well-behaved children. She doesn't respond, just smiles and tucks in. Her soup is getting cold.

As the last of the plates is cleared away, the chef walks into the dining room, balancing their dessert on a long silver tray. He puts it down in the middle of the table, pours a good measure of brandy over it and sets it alight. Chege's guests applaud – banana flambé always impresses. Wairimu strides into the room and leans over Shiro's mother. She whispers quietly, occasionally looking over at Shiro, who is waiting to be served.

'What is it, Wairimu?' Chege asks, in a low voice.

'It's nothing, sir,' she responds and nudges Shiro's mother with her elbow.

'"Nothing" could have waited until our guests left, what do you want?' Wairimu looks down at Shiro's mother for help.

'It really is nothing, son. It's time for Nyambura to eat, that's all.'

'So feed her.' The words are drawn out through clenched teeth. He's embarrassed by the stupid exchange. He turns to Mr Nderitu, 'You must try the bananas with some whipped cream. It's amazing.'

'Sorry, sir,' Wairimu interrupts, 'the door to the nursery is locked.'

Chege stares at her. 'Shiro, please handle it,' he finally tosses over his shoulder.

'Come on, Chege. I thought you were Mr Family Man. Don't tell me you're afraid of mashed peas and *warus*. You handle it,' Mr Nderitu goads.

Chege laughs, 'I'm very hands on, diapers, bathtime, *kila kitu*. Kids are easy. Feed them, clean them, put them to bed. In fact Nyambura has been out for hours. I've missed her, let her meet the people.'

Shiro slowly pulls the key out of her bra and slides it across the table to Chege. He narrows his eyes at her, they will have to talk about that later. He gives it to Wairimu and asks her to cover Nyambura up properly before bringing her down. He doesn't want her to catch a cold.

The banter resumes around the table and Shiro is the first to hear Wairimu screaming, but only because she is waiting for it. As her wails build up to a steady, unbearable moan, the table erupts. Chairs fly, left and right as they all run up the stairs after Chege.

Shiro spoons a generous helping of cream over her bananas. She watches as it drips off her fork and splashes back into her bowl. She closes her eyes as she takes a bite. Chege is right, she thinks. It's delicious.

BM Kunga was born in Nairobi, Kenya in 1986. She is a medical doctor and a writer whose work has appeared in *Kwani?* She is currently working on a collection of short stories.

Bloody Buda

Waigwa Ndiang'ui

AT THE FIRST JUNCTION FROM HIS HOUSE, Buda takes a few cigarettes from Mama Jacinta's shop on credit and almost steps into the gush of water Sam throws out of his barbershop.

'Buda, bloody idiot – watch where you are going. Are you OK?' Sam asks.

'Good, just some idiot tried to give me a bath,' Buda replies.

Buda's dog, Mr Anderson, is wagging his tail at his feet. Buda had found him as a puppy, whining at his doorstep. He'd carried him inside where his sons, who were watching a late-night movie, *The Matrix,* named him after one of the characters. He shoos Mr Anderson away and heads down the road.

He is hoping to meet one of his neighbours, the kind who will stop their car so that he can smile through the window at the Mama Kimani or Mama Mwangi as they say, hey Buda, lucky meeting you, I have some chickens I need slaughtered, or could you paint my house, or trim my hedge, or find me a shamba boy. He needs work. Anything. But it's mid-January and the demand for chicken is low, everyone is broke, worried about school fees and books, and recovering what was squandered in December.

December squander: he slaughtered maybe 20 goats at various parties and more chickens than he can count. That month he was swimming in money and smelling of blood and shit and fat and fur like an inside-out man. When he was not working, he was at Njeri's pub downing mugs of beer and buying jugs for his friends. He makes it to the valley without any offers and listens to a stream gurgling in a culvert under the road.

When he was a boy, the stream was lined with thickets and there was a field of wattle trees to his right where he used to go on hot boring afternoons to get away from those naps his mother forced him to take. He liked to suck on the honey-coloured globs of gum that oozed out of cracked barks of trees and pretend they were sweets. He'd lie on his side next to a fallen tree where no-one on the road could see him, smelling the earth, rotting leaves, and making up stories set in a small crowd of mushrooms next to his head. He loved mushrooms for their earthy smell and the funny shape his mouth took when he said their Kikuyu name: *makuno*. Now, two high-rise flats have come up on both sides of the stream; the thickets and the wattle trees are gone.

He makes his way to the garage where he spends most of his day playing cards, chatting and watching out for work. The garage is behind a row of shops facing the highway. The compound is an obstacle course of vehicles with missing wheels, lights and windshields. There are two other businesses: Gathuri supu base, where you can buy boiled goat's head and soup, and Njeri's Relax bar. Most of the people walking into the compound are headed for the bar. It is the safest place to drink since it became illegal to open bars before five. He walks into the bar's stale-bread stench and can make out a song amidst the shadowy faces and hushed voices. Njeri, the owner, has been cornered by some touts who are trying to get some liquor out of her. One of them is playing her Tupac's *Dear Mama* from his mobile phone, and telling her earnestly that they appreciate her, that she is their mother. Buda hangs his jacket at a corner and joins a card game outside.

Some time in the afternoon, he is eliminated from the game and is scratching his beard, trying to figure out his next move. He has not had a drink. He walks out of the garage to the dual carriageway, runs across the first lanes, jumps over the middle barrier and walks to the other side. This is the poor half of town. The shopkeepers gaze out at nothing while dust rises up the shop fronts as if to reclaim them. The residential section behind the shops is clusters of corrugated iron and wooden houses caught in a web of dirt roads. Progress here has been halted by gravelly, unproductive soil and by Gathuri hill, a rocky steep crag looming above the houses.

Three years ago the town's population doubled when the government set up a camp for IDPs fleeing the fighting in Eldoret. There are a hundred-plus white tents on the far side, forming a cluster as large as the town, and the bleached white tents look like the town's albino twin.

Buda walks to a lane between the shops where Victor is dusting the second-hand clothing he sells. There are faded jumpers and jeans that are still wrinkled from being stuffed into a sack at closing time. Victor is in a stretched purple vest that shows a nipple and a row of ribs when he raises his arm to flick the flywhisk.

'How is it, Buda?' he asks, meeting Buda's fist with his own.

'Not bad, just this bloody sun. Give me the usual.'

Victor dives into one of the sacks and slips a fat joint into Buda's palm.

'I'll give you the money tomorrow.'

'Don't be stupid, Buda, business is bad. I can't start my day giving credit.'

'Come on, man, am I not your customer? Don't I pay? Have I ever run off with your money? You know I can get this thing on the other side, but I risk my life every day crossing that highway to buy your stuff and you won't give me credit on the one day I have no money? You can't be serious.' He throws his hand at Victor and walks away. 'I'll bring you the money tomorrow.'

'Sawa Buda, no problem, but next time ask me first. Tomorrow then.'

'Yeah, if I don't get hit by a car.'

Buda is already thinking about lunch and Rosie's is where he goes when he is broke. It's a small hotel at the end where the town almost touches the camp. There is a kitchen at the back and a 20-foot room at the front where customers wedge themselves into benches and eat with their elbows squeezed to their bodies like praying mantises. There are two benches at the back where one can sit beside the woman doing the dishes and the big boy turning a mountain of *ugali*. There was a time when Buda could get credit at Rosie's, but she doesn't give credit any more. The last time Buda was at Rosie's there was a young man with a bump on his head that, Buda learned from the man seated next to him, Rosie had put there with a *muiko*. Rosie was shouting at him to pay for his food. The man sat staring at Rosie idiotically. Rosie jabbed her finger on the bump and the poor fellow put his face in his hands and moaned.

'I will kill you one day,' she shouted, 'you idiot. I'm not the one who put you in the camp. You think it's my job to feed you people. Get out and never come back.'

There is no point trying Rosie's, so Buda runs back across the road to the garage. Munene, an old friend of his father's, is leaning against the hood of his Peugeot 504. It has a long dent on the driver's side and one of the headlamps is in Munene's hand. Munene's beard is thick and cropped at the cheeks, the same beard Buda's father has in a picture sitting on a curtain box above Buda's dining-room window. Buda shakes Munene's hand and leans on the vehicle to listen to the story. He is telling the mechanics how he ran his car into a tree while trying to escape robbers in Kiambu.

'They kept shouting "men are not your mother" while hitting my knees with a metal bar,' he tells the mechanics.

A few minutes after four, some of the working crowd start to arrive at the bar. When Buda sees King'ori strutting in, pulling the tie from his neck and putting it into his pocket, Buda walks over to him and takes his hand, laughing as he leads him to the bar.

'You look like you ran away from work.'

'Yeah, man, it's Friday – I waited for the boss to go to the toilet and whoosh I was gone.'

'Let's go, you'll buy me a drink.'

'No, no,' King'ori wags his finger at Buda, 'you'll have to earn it at the pool table. Fifty bob a game.'

'You know I'll just beat you.'

Njeri is at a corner. The touts have left and she and her sister are drinking with a pair of police officers, on a table laden with Tuskers and Pilsners. Her face is puffed up and her hair ruffled. She is drunk. Buda says hi to them and goes to the game with King'ori. He wins the first two games and loses the third and fourth. He tells King'ori he will pay him the next day but King'ori will hear nothing of it. Some of the regulars have arrived and they quickly pick up what is going on. Njeri joins the chorus, asking him to pay, and Buda has had enough. He tells King'ori to do whatever he thinks he can do and walks out. He goes to an old toilet behind the bar and smokes half the joint. He takes a few minutes cooling off before he goes back. This time he finds Munene at the counter and manages to get a drink out of him. He goes back to the pool table and sits alone watching the game. He supports Tony because he is a good player and he is playing against King'ori. Someone pats him on the shoulder, and he moves over to let Mwangi slide to the seat next to him.

Mwangi started coming to the club a few weeks ago. He sits alone at a corner with a large mug, that comes up to his eyebrows when he drinks, and a book. He slides past Buda, smiling, and murmurs some niceties Buda doesn't catch. The boys at the pool table have not stopped taking little digs at Buda. He knows they will keep it up until they find some other distraction so he sits with his mug brooding and is surprised when Mwangi taps him on the shoulder again.

'They call you Buda? Like this?' he asks, raising the cover of his book to show him a statue of a fat golden Buddha with his palms brought together under his chin. It takes Buda a minute to recognize what he is looking at. One of the players at the table shouts, 'Ah Buda, don't be like that – you can't just ignore us, pay King'ori his money.'

'Yes,' Buda says patting his belly, 'I am Buddha, and all these bastards bow to me. Leave that one alone, he's mad.'

He takes the book from Mwangi and wedges a fat finger between the pages. He reads the title: *Basic Buddhist teachings: Suffering and enlightenment.* He turns it over, reads the blurb and hands it back to Mwangi. The young man doesn't go back to his reading; he stares at Buda with big doll eyes while his cheeks go up and down a wad of khat tucked under his cheek.

'There are Buddhist stories about meeting Buddha disguised as a beggar or a needy person,' Mwangi smiles, 'It's funny, me reading this book and the guy seated next to me happens to be called Buda.'

He seems to have nothing more to say so Buda goes back to watching the game, where Tony misses an easy shot and the crowd breaks out laughing.

'You can never win with Buda supporting you.' The mad one laughs. 'It's bad kismet.'

'Tony, what the fuck, man, beat this bastard. You hear the way they talk out of their asses. Are you going to let them beat you? Ah, this game is crap,' he says, turning to Mwangi. 'I'd play but I don't have the money. Anyway, why are you reading this stuff?'

Mwangi shrugs. 'I found it at the second-hand book place at the flyover and the title kind of interested me. I don't know,' he adds, a little shy, 'living in the camp puts a lot of questions in your head.'

'That's too much thinking. Buy me a drink and I'll show you how to overcome suffering and be enlightened in two easy steps. Come,' he says. He leads Mwangi to the back of the bar. 'People in this bar amaze me; you got money they are all around you. But once you are broke, they don't even want to see you.' He says this when they are standing against the latrine. He takes out the left-over joint and lights it. 'Now, this is enlightenment. You smoke?'

They smoke in silence passing the joint back and forth until it is a tiny stub that Mwangi deposits in Buda's hand. He pinches it with the tips of his nails and sucks. The evening is golden, the sun is just above the crag on the other side of the road and Buda does not want to go back into the bar. He shows Mwangi to a broken-down Volkswagen and asks for more drinking money. The car reeks of oil and dust and paint but it's cool and quiet and Buda settles in the driver's seat.

'My father owned a Volkswagen,' he says. 'The noise scared my sister to death in the morning.' He chuckles. 'I remember I once told her babies are delivered by a doctor pressing the belly button of a pregnant woman and the belly pops open like the hood of the Volkswagen. All the neighbourhood kids ended up believing that story.'

Mwangi giggles. His little pointy shoulders go up and down and for a minute he can't answer. When he finally speaks, he chokes and coughs out the words, 'I had a sister, she was killed in the fighting.'

'My parents moved to the States with my brother and sisters but I have a wife and two sons here. Let's get another drink,' Buda says, waving the mug in Mwangi's face. Mwangi gives him the money and he comes back with the mugs of beer.

'So are you Buddhists allowed to drink?'

'No. And I'm not a Buddhist,' Mwangi says, pulling a slender stick of weed out of his pocket.

'You've been holding out on me, you little bastard. Let me light it.' Buda sticks it between his lips and lights up. He draws the smoke in and out his cheeks. 'Enlightenment, and overcoming suffering,' he says, holding up the weed then the beer. He pushes out a cloud of smoke and disperses it with his hand.

He reaches over Mwangi and pulls a lever at the base of the seat, reclining it until it touches the back seat. He does the same to his seat and passes the weed to Mwangi. Through the Volkswagen's dusty windshield, the evening star shines in an empty, navy-blue sky. Buda balances his drink on his belly. They sit in silence, each lost in thought. When their mugs are empty, Buda goes to the bar for more. When Mwangi speaks his voice is slurred.

'We lost everything,' the boy seems to continue from somewhere. 'Just look at how massive that sky is, it's crazy to think we matter.'

'You really need to stop thinking. Drink your beer. Relax. It works out in the end.' Buda says. But he is thinking about his mornings, feeding his chicken and rabbits, taking long breaths that dissolve the smell of chicken shit and rabbit urine in his saliva, then sitting at the dining-room table staring at the photos of his parents and siblings standing on the curtain box above the window. He always imagines that he is at a shooting range and they are a firing squad or, if he remembers how one of them annoyed him, he becomes the shooter and they, the targets.

'This is a really nice place to meditate. Do you meditate, Buda?'

This kid is getting too much, Buda thinks. 'I do sometimes,' Buda says,' but you can think until the hairs on your head turn grey. God decides, some people are lucky, some people are unlucky.'

'Buddhists believe...'

'Now wait a minute, enough with all this Buddhist talk.'

'No, no, no – just one little thing. I just wanted to tell you about Karma...'

'That's a lot of nonsense. You are drunk. Can you make it across the highway on your own? Get up, I'll take you.' He pulls his seat up, gets out the door and goes to the other side. He pulls Mwangi's door and the boy stumbles out.

'I can make it out on my own,' Mwangi protests.

The pool table is quiet and there are about five drunks left in the bar. Buda puts his hand around Mwangi's shoulder and they stagger to the main street. It's deserted except for a pair of security guards chatting at a corner. They are almost at the flyover, when Buda sees the silhouette of a police Land Cruiser in the middle of the flyover.

'Mwangi,' Buda shakes the young man, who is leaning heavily on his shoulder, 'Mwangi, Mwangi, we are going to have to cross the road, there's police on the flyover. Can you do it, can you cross?'

'Police, police? Where are they? Where are they? Take me to the police. What can they do, they can't do nothing.'

He tries to break away from Buda and run to the flyover but Buda pulls him back. He leads him down a path that goes to the highway. Three cars zoom past in quick succession. He shakes Mwangi until he gets his attention.

'You can't cross with your eyes closed, you have to be alert, OK?' He looks across the road and pulls the young man to the middle barrier. They jump over and run to the other side. They climb to the shops and begin the walk to the camp. At the bridge, Mwangi sees the police car and shouts: 'We are here, come and get us if you want, you fucking idiots.' The police car remains inert.

'Don't be stupid,' Buda hisses, clutching Mwangi's hand. Mwangi breaks free and runs to the Land Cruiser, shouting.

'Yeah, come on, you cows, arrest us. Where do you think you can take us? You think you are so special?'

A flashlight shines from the back of the Cruiser and sweeps at them. Buda hears the police talking and the thuds of boots. He grabs Mwangi, puts his shoulder in the boy's armpit and runs. The boy is dragging his feet so Buda grabs him by the belt and pulls him off the ground. He can hear the boots chasing and sees flashlights waving around them.

'Simameni,' one of the police orders, 'Afande, shoot them.'

Buda lets go of the boy and stops. The boy drops to the ground. He turns around and raises his hands. Mwangi gets up slowly from the ground. A flashlight blinds them.

'Officer, don't shoot. We surrender,' Buda says. 'Please

forgive my brother, he is a little drunk. I was just taking him home.'

'Shut up both of you and sit down,' the voice behind the flashlight orders. The police stand over them and ask for their IDs. They fish them out.

'I know you, Buda,' the face behind the flashlight says. 'But who is this boy and why is he insulting police officers? You know that is a serious offence?'

'Yes, officer, but understand, he lost his sister the other day and he is drinking too much. It's just the stress.'

'Let him answer for himself. You, you think you can insult the police?' The officer pushes Mwangi's head back. They lower their flashlights and Buda can see dark jackets and G3 rifles strung on their shoulders. 'Look at me.' Mwangi turns his face and gets a loud slap across the face. 'Stand up.' Mwangi gets up slowly, rubbing his cheek. 'Repeat those insults now, eh, where are the insults now?' When his hand leaves his cheek, the officer slaps him again.

'Please, officer, forgive him,' Buda pleads.

'Buda, go. We are going to teach this little idiot who the police are. These are the people who've been causing trouble in the camp.' He pushes Mwangi's face up and slaps him again. Mwangi bends over and puts his face in his hands. One of the officers kicks him and he stumbles to the ground.

'Please, please, officer. I know this boy, he is a good boy, no trouble at all.'

'Buda, you are beginning to annoy us, do you see the Cruiser? Do you want to go to the station? Get out of here. I won't tell you again.'

He gets up and runs across the road. He stands at a shop and can still hear the claps of the officer's slaps. He watches the dark figures with their hands going in and out at the small bundle between them. Then Mwangi wails or laughs – a sound like the braying of a donkey. It only annoys the police and they hit harder. He is quiet. He is on the ground. One of the police grabs the back of his trousers, drags him to the Land Cruiser and throws him in the back. The vehicle revs and they drive off.

Buda watches the vehicle's lights until they disappear. He should have done something to help that poor kid. He looks over to the camp. The tents are peaceful mound-shaped silhouettes in the dark. He was so close. That kid could have been asleep in his tent. Maybe he will go to the police station in the morning, with some bread and milk, if he gets the money.

Waigwa Ndiang'ui was born and lives in Kenya. Two of his short stories, *The Baboon House* and *100% Cotton Day,* appeared in *Kwani? 6.* He is also an Achebe Center for African Writers Fellow. He is currently working on a novel.

Things Are Hard

Yewande Omotoso

FILO GOT UP FROM HER SECURITY STATION, a small wooden table and metal chair with no cushion. She walked to the entrance of the reception area and looked through the glass double doors. The supervisor of Rose-Hope Maternity had asked Filo to stay on duty during the temporary closure of the clinic. One intern was left back and two remaining patients were due to be transferred the following day.

At the sound of her cellphone Filo moved back to the desk. The familiar string of numbers in the window of the phone meant it was from Zim, her sister calling at this crazy hour. Filo let it go to voicemail. It could only be more money that she wanted. Things were hard back home, her younger sister often lamented when they spoke. It was almost five years since Filo had arrived in Cape Town. She had initially applied for jobs as a midwife but her qualifications were scowled at by the various hospital directors who conducted the interviews. They scrunched up their noses at her certificates as if the papers were giving off a funny smell.

'Do you have any reputable referrals?'

They said the word 'reputable' as if they expected she would have an allergic reaction to it.

Eventually, as money got tighter, Filo stopped applying for nursing positions. A friend who worked for a security company found her a job at Rose-Hope. She took it. What is a hard life? Filo wanted to ask her sister. Is it not having the money for new clothes or is it doing nothing with your hands all day, just sitting? Tired, no matter how much rest you get? It is here in this country that things are hard, she would explain. When you come down South you stop being yourself and you start surviving.

Filo checked her watch. She was hungry but she couldn't take a break until the junior intern got back. He'd left a few minutes ago with the excuse of needing a pack of cigarettes. Her phone again. This time she picked up; the line was faint.

'Esther?'

She could barely make out her sister's voice, crowded with static. She moved around the room in search of an elusive clear line.

'You there?'

''Scuse me Nurse?'

Filo looked behind her to see a tall boy standing in the doorway, darkness in the background.

'I have a problem.'

'We are not open, young man.'

Filo brought the phone back to her ear, the line had cleared a bit and her sister was talking.

'Say that again, Esther.'

She raised her hand for the boy to wait but he moved closer.

'I don't mean trouble,' he said. 'I just need your help.'

He had stubble on his chin, uneven, and a clump of angry bumps devouring his jawline. He was definitely on edge about something.

'My girlfriend's pregnant, Nurse.'

Filo held the phone to her shoulder and addressed the boy.

'Look, we're no longer running. They closed down the unit, understand?'

'But she's not well.'

Filo sighed into the phone, 'I'll call you later, there's something happening here. Do you hear me when I say we aren't functioning?'

'But if you can just help me quickly, Nurse. I don't know what else to do!'

Filo looked at her watch, how long had the intern been gone? He was probably taking chances because of the shutdown. Parking off instead of doing his job properly.

'So, can you help me?'

Twenty-two, Filo thought, sizing the boy. Maybe even younger. His skin was yellow, a sick yellow. Filo had done well to ignore it but a stale odour came off his faded green t-shirt.

'What's your name?'

'Phineas. Phineas Adams.'

'Okay, Phineas, what's happened to your girlfriend?'

'I don't know, she's just saying things like she doesn't want the baby.'

'We're not that kind of place. We do not do that here.'

'I know. I didn't mean it like that. She's already six months pregnant.'

'Is she in any pain?'

'I don't think she's in pain. She's not talking about pain. It's just up here,' he grimaced and tapped his temple. 'She's not right in the head, Nurse.'

'What do you mean 'not right'?'

'She just keeps talking to herself, I can't make sense of what she says. I think she's done something to the baby. She just keeps talking about the baby, the baby. Come and see. She's just outside.'

'Why's she outside?' Filo asked.

Phineas pulled Filo towards the door. He was stronger than he looked, with hard hands that gripped like barbed wire.

The air outside was cool. There was one long building that made up the clinic and there was a spiked gate separating the clinic compound from the rest of the Rose-Hope township. Phineas and Filo walked down the short flight of steps. The stoep-light was on. A white blinking light that pulsed over the barren car park. Filo checked her watch, a few minutes past three a.m.

'Magda!' Phineas shouted, as if he thought the girl was deaf.

She sat with her back to them, hunched over. Filo touched her shoulder and the girl shuddered.

'Magda?'

A pair of big eyes took her in for a few seconds, then turned back to studying the ground. The girl's arms were folded over her raised knees and she wriggled her bare toes. She was even more haggard-looking than Phineas, with stringy tawny hair. What would have been a normal pretty face was worn and lopsided. It looked as if someone had taken her face in between the palms of their hands and squashed it. She's on something, Filo thought. Even the boy. He may not have hit for a while but this one, she was definitely coming off some kind of high.

'What's she taken?' Filo asked Phineas.

He feigned surprise and shook his head.

'I need to know what she's taken, Phineas, this could be serious.'

He shook his head again. Filo sighed. Best get the girl inside – the intern would be back soon enough.

'Help me,' she said to Phineas.

He moved down the stairs and took control of one side of Magda as Filo instructed.

'Are we going home?' Magda mumbled. 'If we're going home, then good. 'Cause I'm done here. I've finished with her, we're finished.'

'What is she talking about?' Filo asked.

'The baby,' Magda replied. Her head lolled as they walked her up the stairs and her feet crossed and tangled which meant they went slowly to avoid falling down.

'What's happened to the baby?'

Neither Magda nor Phineas replied. Typical Rose-Hope stuff. Over the years Filo had observed it all from her security desk. Her time working at the clinic had frustrated her. The impotence of her uniform and her stupid security badge. The speckles of grey in her closely cropped hair multiplied. Sometimes, sitting on her chair, Filo watched the emergencies arrive and recited in her head the actions she'd take if it were her case. There was the old woman who came in with her 13-year-old grandchild, the girl big in the stomach, the granny unspeaking, just squeezing her granddaughter's hand. Filo had seen a woman come in ready to give birth – except the bleeding wounds from the thrashing her husband had just given her were almost as pressing a medical matter as the imminent birth of their child. Another woman also in labour and drunk; pushing when she shouldn't and passing out when her co-operation was required. An unsuccessful attempt to abort an eight-week-old foetus had arrived at the clinic once. The woman bleeding, the boyfriend waiting in the car. Filo tried not to, but she judged the doctors on call. And she wrung her hands because she had nothing better to do and she finished her shift.

Back in the reception area, there was a long wooden bench and three other loose chairs that didn't have a permanent place in the room, but moved around depending on what was needed. They put Magda to sit on the bench, the side nearest the wall, so they could lean her head against something.

'Pull one of those up. See that form there, fill it in. I'm going to do a quick examination.'

Phineas scraped one of the metal chairs across and sat in front of Filo's desk. There was a pen and a stack of forms waiting.

Filo used a note pad she kept in her trouser pocket, a pen behind her ear. Relieved that the girl didn't jerk at her touch, she wrote down her observations in short hand. Her pulse rate was up. Quickened heartbeat. Filo checked her temperature and blood pressure. All the vital signs were bad.

'Magda, can we talk for a bit?'

Filo looked into the girl's face. There was a deadness in the eyes; sunken, far gone. The familiar sourness of alcohol as it seeped out the pores.

'Ask about the baby, Nurse,' Phineas whispered from his seat.

Filo snapped a look at him to keep him quiet. He chewed

the tops of his fingers, shaving the nail tips, his face in concentration. The curls of keratin fell to a grey vinyl-tiled floor. He hadn't touched the form.

The girl sat. She was more agitated now than when she'd been outside, her neck twisting at every perceived sound, her eyes popping.

'I got her. I got her,' she kept saying.

Filo stretched her hand out for the form, 'Finished?'

Phineas handed it to her and she frowned.

'You didn't complete this. You have to tell me what drugs she took.'

Filo walked to the desk. She sat down so she could look him in the eyes, level.

'I know it's tik. I'm right, aren't I? Well, is it? And booze too, right?'

He looked at her for what seemed a long while.

'Just nod,' she egged on. 'I can't help you unless I know.'

A small dip and rise of the head. It was a young, lost expression on an old face. His nodding got more and more vigorous, as if he'd gotten over the fear of saying 'yes, we did that'. Water came out of his eyes, he wiped his nose and smeared snot on the back of a hand pocked with bruises.

'How much did she take?'

'I don't know. I'd left. I swear Nurse, I'd left already. We'd stopped, we'd stopped weeks ago. Then I left to try and... to find some... we needed money. So I left and when I came back I found her shaking.'

'She had a seizure?' Filo took down notes on her pad.

'I don't know how much she took.' He rubbed his eyes with his wrist. 'One hit. Two at the most. Couldn't be more.'

'How? She smoke it?'

Something clouded his face.

'Was it a poke?' Filo asked.

He nodded. She'd heard that kids did that these days, shove something up there then fuck their brains out. Her mouth was dry, the room felt warm.

'And you were there, weren't you?'

He paused and then said, 'It was her idea, Nurse.'

'How long ago was this?'

'Around two a.m.'

The number to dial stared back at her from the wall by her security station. The junior intern. But what would he do? Nothing she hadn't done many times over. And better even.

Filo left Phineas and went to Magda. She had to decide what her next action was going to be. If she was right and it was an overdose there was no more waiting time. Who are you kidding, Filo heard the voice in her head talk back at her, you've already decided. She reached towards Magda and the girl screeched.

'It's okay. It's okay,' Filo said.

'They were going to come after her,' the girl screamed. 'I know they were. So I killed her.'

'Let's get her into the ER. Phineas, give me a hand. Magda? Magda?'

The girl's mind had wandered off again. The alertness waned and she was suddenly soft and pliable. Nodding and whispering something. She didn't complain when Filo coaxed her off the bench.

'Take that side,' Filo ordered.

'They wanted to get her so I got her first. Got her away, far away,' Magda rambled as Phineas and Filo bracketed her towards the door.

'You mean the baby, Magda?'

Keep her talking, Filo thought, maybe she'd stay docile long enough for a scan.

'Yes,' Magda answered.

She looked at no-one when she spoke. She looked around at nothing. They walked down a short low passage to halfway and entered a room.

'I took a big big light. A crystal light and I killed her,' she cackled. 'You can't catch me. You can't catch me. You cannot catch me. You cannot catch me. You…'

Filo let Magda perch on the gurney. The girl bounced her body, each pulse to go with the ditty she chanted in a softer and softer tone. Like the end of a song that fades away.

'I killed it,' the girl taunted. 'The baby's dead.'

'Fuck, Magda,' Phineas burst. 'Shit, man!'

'Okay, Phineas. Sit over there and stay quiet. I might need your help… if she fights me. For now, just watch her while I prepare.'

In the small adjoining room Filo washed her hands then looked for the medicine store. She needed something for the seizures. Finding the right bottle, she paused before opening it. She could still call the intern. Just out of diapers that one. Forget it.

'She used the toilet since midnight? Phineas?' she shouted through the open door.

'No.'

Filo collected activated charcoal tablets to empty out whatever toxins still remained in the gut. Her hands shook just a little but she steadied them. She wiped her brow and moved towards the gurney. Filo helped Magda undress. A white vest hardened underneath the armpits. She held Magda's hand as the girl stepped into the hospital blue gown. A toenail was missing.

'Where did you get that?' Filo asked, unable to look away from the gash just beneath her ear.

Had to be something blunt made that cut.

Magda didn't respond.

'Okay, let me help you up.'

Once she settled on the bed, Filo handed her a plastic cup of water and the medication. The girl, thankfully, downed it with no quarrel.

'Now, we're going to get some fluids into you.'

Filo set up the intravenous drip. Her fingers now moved easy as if the years hadn't passed and she was still the busiest nurse in her hometown where she spent her days pressing and rubbing and massaging and holding.

She pricked Magda's skin and the girl didn't seem to feel it. As Filo was taping the tube along the underside of Magda's arm the door of the ER squawked open and she almost wet herself. It was just the wind though.

'Oh Jesus!' she said laughing in fright as she realized she'd been holding everything in. She'd been waiting without thinking about waiting. She now acknowledged the quiet image somewhere in the back of her mind of the intern walking in on a security guard setting up an IV. But it didn't really matter now; there was nothing left but to keep going forward.

Filo moved to hoist up the top of Magda's gown but the girl stiffened, spat at her something thick. She bared a set of demon-like teeth – blackened as if there'd been a fire in her mouth. Filo wiped the spit off her cheek.

'Christ!'

But the girl continued growling so Filo held back. Within a minute the medication started taking effect and Magda's eyes drooped.

'I'm going to do a scan now,' Filo said.

Magda didn't resist when Filo pulled the gown up over the stretched-out belly and she didn't wince at the touch of the gel the nurse had warmed in her hands.

'Let's see,' Filo said turning to look at the monitor.

Filo had kept her pad nearby the entire night. She jotted down what she now saw. Abnormal substances in the amniotic fluid. The fetal heart rate was 220 beats per minute – the baby was alive but severely distressed.

'Everything okay?'

Phineas had stood up and was hovering. He was reading Filo's face, his own contorted with worry.

'Just stay away, I need to work.'

Filo got a stash of pillows and elevated Magda's legs. She wheeled the oxygen tank closer and placed the mask on Magda's face.

'I'm going to have to call the obstetrician… I must call it in. I've stabilized her as best I can.'

Both Phineas and Filo looked at Magda lying on the gurney. Her eyes were closed, her body still and she was breathing deeply. Seconds of quiet passed and then the sound of footsteps coming down the passageway alerted Filo.

'What's going on here?' the intern marched in. 'Get out!' he shouted, assessing the scene and reaching for his phone.

Filo left her medical notes on the side table and pulled Phineas by the hand, out of the emergency room and back into the reception area. The doctor on call arrived soon and very quickly Rose-Hope Maternity was seeing more activity than it had seen in a week. Filo sat back at her security check desk and Phineas was plonked on the bench like a fallen tree. Filo looked out of the double doors. Daylight was coming. She started collecting her few things from the desk. She could feel Phineas watching her movements.

'You going now?' he asked.

Filo nodded. Phineas looked like he wanted to say something else but then he put his hands in his lap and looked away. It was a couple of minutes before he spoke again.

'Will they be fine?'

It was as if the last few hours had added extra lines to his face.

'I think they'll be okay,' Filo said. 'I think we were just in time.'

'Thank you.'

The boy came round to Filo's side. He bent down and leaned into her with his lanky pressing body. Filo held him, she knew how to hold people. She put her hand on the back of his head and stroked.

Yewande Omotoso was born in Barbados in 1980. She grew up in Nigeria and, in 1992, moved with her family to South Africa where she has lived since. Her novel *Bom Boy* was published by Cape Town-based Modjaji Books in 2011. Currently Yewande divides her time between writing her second novel, her profession as an architect and all the other concerns that make up a life.

Pillar of Love

Beatrice Lamwaka

A BOUQUET OF SUNFLOWERS ARRIVES at Lala's door as she parks her Rav 4. She writes her name and signs against it, and asks the deliverer to get out of her sight a.s.a.p. She sucks in the smell of the bouquet. She says, 'Thank you, thank you,' aloud. She raises the bouquet to the sky as if praying to powerful authority. She kisses the flowers. She kneels down on the muddy ground while looking to the sky. She frantically runs to the *matoke** garden where she carefully lays the flowers. She kisses the flowers again and again. Finally, the sign she has been waiting for has arrived. Kaya may be just what she needs.

She runs to the house and heads straight to the spare bedroom. She gets her notebook and records the new number. 'Seven,' she writes in big letters. 'Seven is my new lucky number,' she says. She nods her head and hums 'Feeling Good' by Jennifer Hudson. The lyrics of the song suit exactly how she feels: 'A new day, a new life for me. And I am feeling good.' Kaya has kept his promise and she likes the new feeling it arouses in her. She plucks off the card and burns it. 'Grace mustn't see this. I must keep this a secret,' she says.

She hasn't received flowers from Grace in a year. She reads the name and the message on the card again. It says: 'See you later, Kaya.' She met Kaya some time ago at a party. He has been sending her flowers since then. She noticed him because he recited poetry. She loves poetry recital. Whenever

* Plantain

she hears of poetry performances, she goes. She hopes to write poetry one day. And Kaya resonates the poetry in her and her dreams to become a poet. Kaya is a tall man with perfect white teeth. She needs a man like that to make her feel good about herself. She has been feeling low for a while. These days, she feels her spirit going down by the end of day. There has been nothing eventful happening to her. She has wanted to dodge her friends because they always ask what is new in her life and there has been nothing to tell them. She has realized that she no longer laughs like she used to.

She wants to spend more time with men now. The two years she has been living with Grace have clouded her dreams of children, and Grace does not seem bothered by that. Lala had hoped to have children by 24 but now, at 26, her womb is yearning to bear fruit. She hopes that her dinner date with Kaya will go well. He may be the man that changes her mind about her relationship with Grace. She will have to be at her best. She will wear a short dress to expose a bit of her legs. She will have to show him something for him to appreciate. Her mother always told her that men were shallow. She would have to work hard for them to notice and appreciate her. Her short dress would tell him what she was interested in. There was no need for her to hide this desire.

Lala has always been a moralist, doing what is right. She has never cheated on Grace but she feels the strong urge to be with a man. What if she wasn't meant to be with a woman? What if Grace wasn't right for her? Going out with Kaya would answer some of these questions. If this date turns out bad then she will not go out with anyone but Grace, she thinks. She had never really dated anyone. Grace was her best friend, and the person she felt comfortable with. She could not imagine her life without Grace. And when Grace asked her if they could get married, she didn't think twice about it. It was easy: they could get a few friends and a bible. They had shared intimate moments many times. They were soon married because they could not live without each other. But now, she wanted to know what was out there – what her chances with other people were.

Grace would never allow her to see a man. They had boyfriends but Grace would never allow her to spend time with them without her. Lala will tell her she is going out for poetry in session. Grace does not like to sit and listen to people recite poetry. 'I can read poetry, why should I sit through and listen to somebody ramble on?' she would say when Lala asked her to go out with her. As long as it was poetry night, Grace wouldn't ask where she was going; that is why she agreed to go out with Kaya on a Tuesday night.

She washes her hands and starts to cook the evening meal. 'Maybe I should tell Grace I need a break,' she murmurs as she peels potatoes. 'An "open relationship", like people put on their statuses on Facebook.' She didn't know what it meant to tell people about her relationship. She could not openly tell people that Grace was her partner. Her Facebook status was single and men sent her romantic messages. Sometimes she flirted with them. But she didn't take this as a crime against her relationship with Grace.

She knows that a conversation with Grace about a break-up will not be easy. Between peeling potatoes and stirring meat stew, she rehearses what she will tell her. 'I want a divorce because my parents will kill me.' She shakes her head. 'Because… many gay couples have been killed.' She shakes her head. 'Because…' At the end, she is not convinced by the words she comes up with. She thinks of writing a poem to let Grace know what she thinks but she gives up the idea. She hears Grace's car and she wipes her mouth as if she has been caught stealing sugar.

As soon as Grace sits on the sofa with her matoke crisps, Lala mutters, 'Grace, it would be nice if we got a break from each other – like date other people.' She had not intended to add the part about dating other people. She wishes that she could take back the words but they float in the room as if to haunt her. Grace stares at her. She looks her up and down like she has lost her mind. They remain silent for a while. 'I want a divorce,' Lala says. She looks at her feet. Her toenails are chipped – she will need to go to the salon soon.

'There is no such a thing as divorce in our case,' Grace answers. She does not take her eyes off the TV. She continues eating matoke crisps. Her dreads are neatly twisted. She is the tallest girl Lala has ever met. Lala was attracted to her tallness. Her sisters and brothers are all taller than her and she always wanted a tall girl friend. And when she met Grace in school she didn't hesitate to tell her about her admiration. They have been best of friends since high school. They have visited each other's homes and she had spent Christmas with Grace's family. They had spent nights in Grace's bed in their family home, with nobody suspicious of anything. To both their parents, Grace and Lala were best friends. Lala's parents were happy that their daughter had such a wonderful friend who ate *malakwang* and *kal*. And Grace's family were happy that Lala could peel matoke.

'I am tired of this kind of life,' Lala says. Ever since she met Kaya, she has been seeing new possibilities: a man, children. Lala was not attracted to Kaya but the possibility that she could have children with him made her think about him. She had heard friends talk about how men had vowed that, given an opportunity, they would make them love only men and never think of their partners. One of their gay male friends had a whole church praying for him. After a while, when they didn't see him hold a girl's hand on the way to church, they left him to do what he wanted. He now lives with his partner.

As a young girl, Lala had dreamt of a white wedding. She used to smile at tall boys she thought she might marry one day and hoped to have four little boys. She had all their names in her journals. Each year, she addressed her thoughts to one of them.

'We could adopt children, you know,' Grace says, as if she has read Lala's mind. Lala knows that Grace does not want to have children. She says that she is too messed up to have a 'mini her'. Grace continues to watch NTV. She chews matoke crisps louder. She hums 'Bloom Bloom', a church song she learnt in school.

'First tell your parents that you are married to me, then we shall have this conversation again,' Grace says. She picks up her plate, walks to the kitchen and dumps the remainder of her matoke crisps in the dustbin.

Lala stares at the TV. She does not understand why Grace still wants this marriage. Although they still sleep in the same bed, they no longer hug and kiss as they used to do. Grace always stays late at work. When she comes home, she spends all evening watching TV. The last time they went to Serena Hotel for dinner was six months ago. They only have papers from their lawyer friend to show that the marriage actually happened. Their wedding was witnessed by their gay friends. The marriage, something she dreamt would be witnessed by many, otherwise passed unnoticed. That day, Lala had cut her finger, mixed her blood with that of Grace as a sign of love and vowed that they would live together till death. She wondered if that bond could be broken. Perhaps they should have left some leeway just in case.

'No, I just want to start all over again,' Lala says. She could walk away and never come back and Grace would not have claim to her. They are a couple only to themselves. Nobody would argue in court that they were actually married, since gay marriages are illegal in Uganda. She does not have the strength to leave but Lala thinks that one day she might. She might marry a Kaya and have children. All her school friends have children and when they meet her they touch her stomach and ask her if there is something there. She wants something to be there next time a friend asks. Saying 'no, nothing' for almost five years has taken its toll on her.

She does not eat the food she has just cooked. She hopes that Grace will serve herself when she is gone. She doesn't bother to tell her about the food. She showers and wears a black dress; it will make her seem smaller, she hopes. Dinner at 9pm is a bit late for her. She prefers to eat at 6pm. Kaya stops work at 8pm so there was no way she was going to get him to come early.

'I am going out for poetry in session,' she says as she walks out of the house. Grace nods but says nothing.

Lala is eager to meet Kaya, to see him in a different light. The last time they spoke on the phone, he had recited for her Derek Walcott's 'Love After Love'. She likes that poem. But she was not sure it was one of her favourite poems after he was done reciting it to her.

She has not been in a man's company in a long time. She always wanted someone who was deep. And she found the depth in Grace. Grace knows what Lala wants to say before she says it. She knows what Lala feels after an incident. Grace's intelligence and her ability to understand her were the things she could never get enough of. Lala relied on her to fill in the gaps when her mind went blank. Every time she went out, Grace was with her. It was Grace who spoke most of the time as Lala tried her best not to contradict her.

She arrives before Kaya. She looks out for him but, when she does not see him, she chooses a corner table facing the door. She looks around in the restaurant just in case she finds a familiar face, but does not see anyone she knows. She does not want somebody to tell Grace they saw her with a man. She picks up her journal and begins to write the day's events. She scratches her head to remind her of something brilliant that may have happened, but there is nothing worth recording. She checks her phone for missed calls. Nobody has called her or sent her a text message.

Having children would bring some action into their life. These days their life was boring and Lala wanted something to happen. Two years of just her and Grace was not enough. There were no surprises any more. Dinners out were just routine. The exchange of gifts was what they had been doing since they met. Lala wanted something more and she thought children would bring joy and peace in their home. They would have to deal with homework, the challenge of paying school fees. The things their straight friends talked about. She wanted to share that experience too. For now, she could only talk about the gifts Grace brought home, the places they had gone on holiday. Nobody talked about that any more. They spoke about children, how blessed they were to have children. Little ones running around in the house. The intelligent things they said. She wanted that feeling too.

Kaya arrives with a sunflower. 'I am sorry, I am late,' he says. He is six feet and he towers over her. She smells his aftershave. She knows he freshened up before he came. She likes the way he flashes his white teeth when he smiles. She offers him a handshake but he ignores it.

'That's very Ugandan of you. I should have called before I left home.' Lala stands up to hug him. He hugs her tightly. She feels his rough stubble on her face. She feels his warmth. She likes the body contact. 'I could do this forever,' she thinks. She gently pushes him away. She has been that close to a man. She sits down and he sits opposite her and stares into her face.

'You smell nice,' she says.

'Thanks. You are so warm. Can I get another hug?'

'Each hug costs a million. Are you willing to pay?' She laughs.

'Oh, sure. I hope you like this restaurant. They cook only local food. I don't like fast food.'

'This is fine.'

A waitress brings him a menu. 'Rice and meat,' she says.

'Same,' he says without looking at the menu. Grace hates people who order exactly the same food as she does. Lala often makes sure she orders exactly what she wants to eat.

Kaya recites for her Austin Bukenya's 'I Met a Thief':

I met a thief, who guessed I had
An innocent heart for her to steal.

He stops suddenly, as if not sure of the next stanza. She is still impressed he can remember the words of the first stanza. He holds his knife like he going to slaughter his rice. As he recites poetry, food from his mouth spits in her plate. She stops eating her food and watches him. He does not stop to ask if she is enjoying his performance.

When the waitress hands him the bill she insists on paying her part.

'They always give the men the bill,' she says.

'Men pay the bills, remember,' Kaya says.

Lala does not like men with such attitudes. She has always complained to Grace about such men's attitudes. 'This is the 21st century,' she murmurs.

'Don't kill my manhood. I hate women who think they can do it because they have money.'

'Get serious. I am paying for my part and forget it.' She gets a 20,000-note from her wallet and leaves it on the table. She does not care that that money can pay for both their meals. She wants to get away from him as fast as she can. 'Bastard,' she says as she walks out of the restaurant.

He recites from 'Song of Lawino' by Okot p' Bitek:
Now you treat me with spite
And say I have inherited the stupidity of my aunt.

She ignores his words and heads straight for her car. She will need to think about what has just happened before she gets home. She hopes she finds Grace asleep.

Lala feels like the dinner with Kaya was a waste. She smells her clothes to gauge whether his aftershave has remained on her. All she can smell is her perfume. She picks up the sunflowers she had thrown in the matoke garden. She wipes them clean with her scarf. She sucks in the smell of the bouquet. Sunflowers are her favourite flowers. She loves the bright yellow and the fact that they turn to face wherever the sun is. 'That is how I am with Grace – where she is, I will follow,' she says. She kisses the flowers.

Lala finds Grace watching TV. She hands her the bouquet.

'With love from Lala,' she says.

'Thank you, my dear.' Grace takes the flowers and puts them in a vase. She returns and places it on the table. They both look at the flowers.

'Come sit with me,' Grace says, as she makes space for her on the sofa. Lala flops on the sofa. Grace covers her with the khanga she has been covering herself with. It is not cold but Lala appreciates the closeness to Grace's body. She hasn't been this close in a long time. They remain silent for a while. Lala can hear Grace's heartbeats.

'Don't ever say you want to divorce me,' Grace says as she puts her head on Lala's shoulder. 'We can go through this; you know, adopt a baby or something.'

'I know,' Lala says.

Beatrice Lamwaka was born in Gulu in northern Uganda, and now lives in Kampala, Uganda. She is the Treasurer of the Uganda Women Writers Association (FEMRITE) and a freelance writer with the newspaper *Monitor* and Global Press Institute. She is currently studying an MA in Human Rights at Makerere University. She won the 2011 Young Achievers Award in the category of Art, Culture and Fashion. She was Laureate for Council for the Development of Social Science (CODESRIA) Democratic Governance Institute 2010. She was shortlisted for the 2011 Caine Prize for African Writing and was a finalist for the PEN/Studzinski Literary Award 2009, and received a fellowship from the Harry Frank Guggenheim Foundation in 2009. She has worked as a researcher and teacher in Uganda; and she worked with an international humanitarian agency in Italy and Sudan.

Notes from Mai Mujuru's Breast

Tendai Rinos Mwanaka

THEY WERE BUSY DIGGING when, all of a sudden, the police dog was upon them. It was a huge wild animal baring its fangs in Chris's face, baying for his warm blood. Chris tried to fend it off but it got his hand in its jaws. Chris bellowed with pain. Daniel had run on but when he heard Chris crying he stopped and turned to look back. He catapulted back into the battle lines without a thought for his own safety, grabbed a stick and beat the dog on its hind legs. The dog yelped as it let go of Chris's hand. Chris was up in an instant; he picked up his pack of soil and ran on towards the mountains. The police were now behind them, chasing them. The two men ran harder, but Chris was not such a good runner so the dog rammed into him before he could get clear. He fell down in a heap and the dog was on top of him, trying to bite his throat, but Chris was fast this time. He gripped the dog's neck. He couldn't crush his hand around its throat to suffocate it and barely held it off as they wrestled on the ground.

When Daniel realized that Chris was going to be devoured by this monster, he dropped his pack of soil where he was, grabbed a big stone and made for the battlefield again. When he was near, he took aim at the police dog and let the stone go in one powerful throw. The dog collapsed beside Chris. As Chris tried to rise from his position he heard the *cluck cluck boom* of an AK47 nearby. He looked around and saw Daniel sliding down as the bullets burned into him.

He knew that if he tried to run he would be dead meat, so he started slithering along the ground like a snake, gripping handfuls of grass, roots and rubble. It was a distance of 50 metres to the forest; he pushed through like a possessed man. Some would have given up, but Chris had to survive to tell the story, for Daniel and the other people who had died at the hands of the police here in Marange. He felt the darkness enveloping him. It was night; it seemed he was really dreaming...

He had survived before in this place. Five years ago, he was a young, level-headed man when his girlfriend Concillia asked to meet him under the baobab tree, in the western fields of Marange. They were out there for their annual Passover. It was their spiritual home, where their church originated, so every year they would make a pilgrimage to this area. He had grown up in this church, and found love in it. He and Concillia had promised to marry each other after this Passover. They were hoping for a revelation from God on their impending marriage.

As he was walking towards the fields that morning, he couldn't help noticing winter was setting in, colouring everything a grey, brownish colour, and the fields were bare of crops. Winter always made him feel anxious, as if he was about to lose everything, or maybe it was the tone in Concillia's voice.

'I want to talk to you, Chris.'

'Talk? About what, Concy?'

'I think we should stop seeing each other. It's God's revelation.'

'We haven't consulted the Prophet. I don't understand you, Concillia.'

'There is something that happened to me yesterday, Chris. I was praying under this tree in the morning, as I had been told to do by Prophet Madzibaba Johanne Wechipiri. In the church, last Saturday, he prophesied to me that I should go to the baobab tree and pray for our relationship. He said God would give me a revelation. I did as I had been told and was praying fervently when God bellowed in a huge voice from up the tree, telling me: "Your prayers are heard, young woman." I replied, "Say what you want to say, God, your servant is listening".'

'How did you know it was God speaking?' asked Chris.

'It was God, speaking in the voice of our Prophet Madzibaba Johanne Wechipiri.'

'What if it was Madzibaba himself speaking?'

'No. it was God, God speaks through prophets, Chris. Please stop blaspheming the spirit of God.'

Contritely, he asked her, 'And what did he say?'

'He told me I was set aside for a great promise. I was going to conceive a prophet for the church; and this son of mine will be the son of the current prophet, Prophet Madzibaba Wechipiri. So, Chris, I have to marry the Prophet.'

Now, as he drifted in the dream, he saw Concillia. She was pregnant, and it was with the third child in five years, but she was groaning and groaning. Maybe he felt her groans in his own groans. She was struggling to give birth and his mind told him she was dying. He didn't feel he had to save her. There was nothing he could do about it all.

When Chris realized that he had lost his love to the Prophet, he was so devastated that he stopped going to the church altogether and started drinking himself crazy. His best friend Daniel told him he had to let go, but he couldn't. He knew deep down there was a conspiracy. Young men in this church had always been second choice for girls. Young people were not allowed to be prophets. Even when they were in the church, the girls were told to sit facing the old married men, while the boys and young men were told to sit facing old women. Daniel had also had his girl taken; now it was Chris's turn.

After the end of the pilgrimage, their group left for Nyatate, but Chris didn't go back with them. Even though Daniel tried to convince him to go back with the others, he refused. He parted with his friend. He stayed on in Marange. A couple of months later, when he realized he had no recourse to God, and that he was drinking himself into a wreck, he left for the city of Harare to stay with his uncle. He also started dealing with the drinking bouts.

Over the following five years, he drifted from one relationship to another, one job to another. This was now the situation; it seemed that it was so for the whole country. He didn't have money, but nobody had money. It was at the height of the political problems in the country. People were scuttling all over the country trying to eke out an existence. Not surviving, no. One couldn't even think of living, no. One just had to exist.

When he came to, Chris was on his stomach at the edge of the mountain. Everything was quiet. He touched his throbbing hand and remembered what had happened. He rose slowly, afraid of attracting those bloody dogs and the police. He looked down to the killing fields below and when he was sure there was no-one there he started walking back to where they had killed Daniel.

Marange had changed him again. Growing up, this name Marange had meant something totally different to Chris. It had meant something so pure, so holy.

But Marange is a wilderness. In actual fact, Marange is a bloody pit. The hot air blows like a stoked blast furnace year round. You can't grow crops other than *rapoko* and *mhunga*, which sometimes don't get beyond germination. When diamonds were discovered, the whole community thought it was a spiritual gift for the people of Marange as absolution for the recurring droughts in this place. For some time, they were inhospitable to people coming from other areas. But it didn't take too long before it became a Mecca for the rest of the country. Then the authorities butted in, in their usual grab-and-plunder way.

A few months before the whole country descended on it, those Johanne Marange sect members had returned to Marange for their annual Passover. It was at the height of the cholera epidemic that swept through the country. It wiped out Chris's clan members. Now, he was back here too: but not to exhume the bones of his family members buried in Marange soil, no.

Chris phoned his old friend Daniel when he decided to take this journey and asked him to join him in the endeavour. Daniel had agreed, but mostly because he just wanted to see his friend, whom he hadn't seen in over five years.

He had taken a train to Mutare to meet Daniel so that they would approach Marange from the side which was less guarded, rather than by the direct road from Harare. They were taken by a big truck to Chipinge, and then ferried on to Chikohwa. Then they walked by foot, a distance of over 50 kilometres, crossed Odzi River and arrived at Marange at about six in the evening. On the way, they plotted their adventure together.

'Those guys over there are saying that the whole place, the whole Marange diamond fields, has been parcelled into four parts. The first part is known as Mufakose.' They were reclining under a hulking mimosa tree, off the road, across from Chiadzwa shops. Mufakose means, 'to die in everything', thought Daniel, but he said: 'Yes, this is the place where we get the *ngodas*.' A ngoda is a poor, cheap form of diamonds, an 'industrial' diamond.

'Like Mufakose Township hugs the industrial area in Harare!' Daniel quipped.

'It hugs the industries for sure.'

'Behind that river, they are saying that place is known as Mbare.' Also named after a notorious high-density slum in Harare.

There were waiting for the night to be darker so that they could invade the fields with the others sleeping, loitering, talking, all around Chiadzwa shops. They knew they could only get into those two places, Mufakose and Mbare. There were two other parts they couldn't invade. The third part was known as Mbada, named after the leopard, perhaps because of the beauty of the 'glass' diamond found in this spot. The fourth part was known as Zamu raMai Mujuru: 'Mai Mujuru's Breast'. The Mujuru family were mining this area. Chris and Daniel couldn't help laughing at this: the people still had a sense of humour. But another thought came to Chris's mind. A breast to a little kid or even to an old man represents life, living, loving.

Mbada area and Mai Mujuru's Breast were fenced off, with the police, the army, the intelligence and the Green bombers doing 24-hour guarding of the place. The police didn't want anyone near Mai Mujuru's Breast, and Mufakose and Mbare were too close. The government wanted everyone to go back to the actual Mufakose and Mbare townships, in Harare, over 300 kilometres away. So the battles in Mufakose were like a country at war. Chris, Daniel and the other people would stay away from the area during the day, and sleep at the nearby Chiadzwa shops. A lot of people were killed; in fact, while Chris was there, he witnessed at least five deaths every day. People were also being beaten up by the police; some were eaten alive by the police's dogs. Some had devised a new method to deal with the dogs. When they were being chased they would lead the dogs far away from the police, and then they would stone the dogs to death or give them poisoned meat. And the battles continued.

But still, everyone kept digging in the Mufakose or Mbare areas. The whole country was staying in Mufakose, mining whatever little ngodas they could scrounge, eking out an existence. But some poor people developed ambitions. Some couldn't abide the idea of staying in Mufakose for the rest of their lives.

And what did they do about it? They started foraging beyond the pig-fence wire that surrounded Mai Mujuru's Breast. Inside the fence, Zamu raMai Mujuru was made up of heaped-up mounds of the coveted glass diamond and soil. If you were to lick a bit of that breast, you would go home smiling and vault yourself out the Mufakose Township into the lush, leafy northern suburbs of Harare.

'So, Chris, are we going to taste Mai Mujuru's huge mounds?' Daniel asked.

'We don't have the money to bribe the police on duty,' said Chris. 'It isn't possible for everyone, man. The sums they are demanding are so huge.' One policeman was found with US$44,000 after an eight-hour guard duty. There was a lot of money involved. Chris and Daniel had used up everything they had on transport from home.

What it meant for them, and for most Mufakose residents, was that they had to stay down there, beside the industries with the 'industrial' diamonds. Those with the money would be given under an hour to get in, through the gates or by cutting the wire, grab a piece of Mai Mujuru's Breast and get out before capture. The bribed police would sound off a warning by blasting their rifles into the air, and the bribers would know they had to run from Mai Mujuru's abundance. The bribed police would only appear if their superiors were coming to inspect them, or after the hour of foraging was up.

'An hour should be plenty time to make love to Mai Mujuru!' Chris said, sizzling with laughter. Daniel was grinning.

'Yes. Those who get rich from Marange, it seems, get rich doing this. Those who will remain poor will stay in Mufakose and Mbare.'

It was tough but they knew it was the truth. They had very little chance, but they had come, so they had to try. They had to dance around the police.

'I still don't know how we are going to see the diamonds in this dark night. Are we going to use candles, or maybe torches? Or maybe we could use our cellphones.'

Chris gave Daniel another empty five-kilogram pack before answering him. 'No, we don't use torches. The police would see us straight away and we would be dead meat. What we'll do is dig some soil and pack it in this plastic, and then tomorrow morning we will wash it with water and find whatever is there.'

The first day, they entered the area at around 8 at night. Before they started digging, they heard the *cluck cluck* sounds of the AK47 as the killing orgy started, so they ran into the nearby mountains with the little soil they had dug and waited for the police to leave the area. An hour later, they returned to the fields. The police came back, and Chris and Daniel ran off. They returned a little bit later and continued digging for the ngodas. That first day they did all that with no success. The second day, they tried again and got nothing. But they didn't tire. The third day they tried again, got their five-kilogram packs filled up with soil, washed it on the morning of the fourth day, and Chris found his first ngoda. He sold it for Z$600 billion dollars, and bought food. Only bread and milk! But it was a welcome relief. They had their first real meal in over three days. Galvanized by the food, that fourth day they went into the fields again – nothing. They became more and more desperate. So, on the fifth day, that's when they tried invading the fields during daylight and met with tragedy.

Now Chris was alone. It was only a few days ago when they'd been so geared up to earn a living through this illegal mining endeavour. Now he had to confront the evidence of their failure. Meat flies were now gorging themselves on Daniel's hot blood, dripping as if from everywhere. He stood there transfixed for some minutes. He couldn't even bow down and howl in grief.

He knew he couldn't raise Daniel from the dead. He had to

continue living for the sake of Daniel, who had sacrificed his life to save him. So, he took his friend's shoes, his watch and cellphone. He took the packets of soil and left Daniel there. He knew the bastards who had killed Daniel would come back later with their vehicles and cart his remains off the fields for burial in the same graveyard where his clan members who had died from cholera were buried. He would not visit Daniel in his final resting place. He wouldn't even be able to identify him, for they never put inscriptions on those graves. The following morning he washed the two packs with water and found nothing.

The bread and milk were done with. He couldn't think of spending more days eating wild fruits. Rather, he sold Daniel's worn-out shoes, Daniel's spare shirt, their cellphones and Daniel's watch.

At Beitbridge, he bribed some border gangsters to help him cross into South Africa illegally. He was stripped of any loose change and abandoned just after crossing the Limpopo. He had to find his way through by foot to Musina refugee camp. He processed a refugee permit worth only six months and became one of the refugees.

Chris hasn't been to his rural home for years – almost six years now. Marange doesn't remind him of his childhood any more, but of the foraging, fondling, caressing of Mai Mujuru's Breast and the death of his friend Daniel. He has never returned home to see those of his clanspeople left behind after the cholera scourge. He has never seen his beautiful Concillia, whom God stole from him through the Johanne Marange sect. He knows that she died during a difficult pregnancy. He hasn't seen his parents for years either. He later heard that the Mujurus were still there, hidden under other names. Nowadays, there is only one name being heard in Marange: Mbada Diamond Mining Company. Maybe the beast Mbada had suckled all the milk in Mai Mujuru's Breast.

Tendai Rinos Mwanaka was born in 1973, in the village of Mapfurira village in Nyanga district, and now lives in Chitungwiza, Zimbabwe. Author of the poetry collection, *Voices from Exile* (Lapwing Publications, Northern Ireland, 2010) and the novel *Keys in the River: Notes from a Modern Chimurenga* (Savant books and publications, March 2012, US).

African Violet

Rehana Rossouw

THERE'S AN AFRICAN VIOLET ON MY DOORMAT; its purple flower peeping out between the dark green leaves. It's in a brown plastic pot, with a base to catch the water. There's no card. It hasn't fallen off, or slipped under the mat. Who knows my address? Did I post it on Facebook when I moved in yesterday?

An African Violet is such an old lady plant. Gogo had a row of them in clay pots on her kitchen windowsill. They had a summer home in her lounge; sunshine burned their leaves to crepe paper. I stroke the furry leaves; they're as soft as Gogo's cheeks.

I've never owned a plant before. What am I supposed to do with it? All I know is that it doesn't like the sun and it likes kitchen windowsills. I don't know if the sun shines into my kitchen. I set a reminder on my phone to check on the plant before I leave for work tomorrow. How much water does it need? Google will know.

It's cute. I like it. It looks small and alone on the long sill above the sink; I should get another one to keep it company. Who sent it? Gogo would definitely have chosen a plant as a house-warming gift; she was big on young people taking responsibility. It's been almost a year since she died but her voice is still loud in my head. I've been talking back these past few months; too excited about buying my first home not to share all the details with her.

I'm not sure Gogo would approve of some of my choices. She expected me to join a law firm that fought for human rights. I tried that for two years after graduation but my clients' problems gave me frightened nights. My new position in the mergers department at a top Sandton firm suits me fine.

My new home is perfect. It's a world away from the Soweto street where I grew up with Gogo after my mother's passing – its fences were low enough for everyone's business to climb over. My complex, less than five kilometres from my office, has high walls protected by an electric fence and security guards at the boom gates.

How did the plant get past all of that and onto my doormat? Did the person who brought it knock to check if I was home? I don't have a peephole in my door, or a chain; two more things to add to the never-ending list of things to do around here.

I know what to do! Visitors have to sign in before they can get into the complex. The intercom has a button marked 'security', I don't have to go out to the gate.

'Hello, security.'

'Lerato Magashule here, in unit number four. Was there a delivery for me today? Do you keep records?'

'Let me check, Madam. I will call you back.'

I lean against the passage wall and check my Facebook page on my BlackBerry while I wait. I haven't posted my new address, but I have changed my status to 'Living in my own home for the first time'.

The intercom shrills in my ear.

'Hello Madam. Emmanuel here, from security. There was no delivery for you today.'

* * *

There's a plate waiting on my doormat when I get home from work. Filled with yellow curls of dog poo. Omigod! I freeze to a halt with one foot on the top step and one foot on the landing. Who put it there? Why? I force myself closer and find the pluck to look down onto the plate. It doesn't smell bad. What is it?

Koeksusters! I'm such a fool! Where did I get the idea it was dog poo? I carry the plate into the kitchen, lifting the cling wrap and sniffing the sweet shine of the syrup on the plaited dough. Halfway through my first bite my eyes fall on the African Violet that arrived yesterday. It seems happy on the windowsill. The purple flower is a cocktail umbrella planted in the centre of the mossy leaves.

I spit the sweet pulp onto the plate and stare at the mess I've made. Who put the plate on the doormat? Why is there no note again? What to do? Security's no help. I fold my arms and stroke my hands from my elbows to my shoulders. I don't want this feeling in my new home; not when I'm living alone. I know this fear. It came with the last case at my old firm, chasing me into the safe arms of commercial law.

The unit next door shares the landing with me. Maybe my neighbours saw something. I'm going to find out. There isn't much wall between the neighbours' door and mine. I haven't heard a thing from their side since I moved in, not even a television voice. I knock. A minute or two later there's a voice, so soft that it disappears as it passes through the door.

'Hello?'

I put a smile in my voice. 'Hello? It's Lerato Magashule here, your new neighbour.'

I hear locks clicking. The door opens a crack. I have to look down to find a face; it's at child's height. I keep my smile and stretch out my hand.

A skinny hand grips the door and opens it slowly. Dark blue veins swell under thin skin as it stretches out towards mine.

'Pleased to meet you. I'm Dorothy Walker. I have been listening out for you, but you are as quiet as a mouse.'

'Um, Ms Walker? I have a problem, and I was hoping you can help me?'

'Please, come inside. And call me Dorothy.'

Her unit's the mirror image of mine. There's a creamy beige carpet on the lounge floor. The walls are white and empty.

The only furniture is a pine trestle table and a computer chair. On the trestle is an iMac pro, with a 27-inch screen and wireless keyboard – exactly the one I picked out at the Apple Store that I'm collecting on payday. I walk over and stroke the monitor.

The voice behind me is a little stronger. 'It's a lovely machine. The resolution is fabulous.'

Dorothy's wearing white nylon school socks. Her pink and white Hello Kitty pyjamas can't be more than age ten to twelve. Her looks put her anywhere between forty and seventy. There isn't a line on her face although her hair is as white as her walls.

'Um, Dorothy, I was hoping you can help me with a problem?'

She doesn't look interested. I speak fast; get my story out before I'm sent on my way. 'I found a potplant at my door yesterday; and a plate of koeksusters tonight. There was no note, both times. It's starting to freak me out. Did you see or hear anything?'

Dorothy lifts her hand to her mouth. Her thin, pale eyebrows stretch up towards her widow's peak. Her voice quivers. 'My dear, I'm so sorry. That was me. I ordered the gifts online for you. I should have thought about a card. I should have been more considerate.'

I feel terrible. This is my first neighbour and I'm accusing her of freaking me out.

'I'm sorry. I should have thought before I...'

Dorothy's raised hand silences me. 'Now that I think about it, you have every right to be scared. That was such a stupid, stupid thing I did. Will you ever forgive me?'

How can I not? Gogo would have made a cake with her own hands and taken it to new neighbours the day they moved in. I accept the cup of coffee and koeksuster Dorothy offers.

✽ ✽ ✽

The shower's running. Did I leave it on? I showered when I got home. That was hours ago. I didn't hear it while I sat with my laptop in bed afterwards, preparing for tomorrow's hearing. It definitely wasn't running full blast when I fell asleep.

Oh shit! Ohshitohshit! Where's the water coming from? Where do I turn it off? Fuck! It's hot! What to do, what to do?

I run outside in my nightie and pound on Dorothy's door till my knuckles burn. I hop up and down on the landing while I wait for her, waving my hands limply in front of my breasts. There's steam leaking through my front door.

Dorothy opens. She's in her Hello Kitty pyjamas, her thin hair standing up in all directions.

Words pour out of me like the waterfall in my bathroom. 'There's hot water coming out of the ceiling and I can't work out how to stop it. Please come help.'

I'm halfway down my passage before I realize Dorothy isn't following. I turn back. She's still planted in her doorway, her arms folded like a skinny wrestler.

'Dorothy?'

'I think I know what the problem is. Your geyser has burst. Phone security, they know where to turn off the water. I will wait up for you; let me know how it turns out.'

Her door closes in my face.

Emmanuel is on duty. He comes quickly and finds the water mains at the bottom of my small patio garden. The waterfall slows to a trickle, and finally it stops.

I mop up the water and dry the floors until I'm exhausted. I have to be up at five o'clock, two hours from now, to drive to Pretoria before the highway jams up into a parking lot. My foot has left the ground to start my crawl into bed when I remember Dorothy is waiting to hear from me.

I knock softly, but she opens on the second knock.

I don't have the energy to greet. 'Emmanuel says it is the geyser.'

Dorothy nods. 'Phone your insurance company tomorrow and get them to repair the damage.'

'I don't have insurance. It's on my list of things to do. Fuck! How much is this going to cost?'

Dorothy's see-through hand clutches mine. 'Don't worry lovey, I have a good plumber. I will have him call you and give you a quote.'

'I can't do anything tomorrow. Or the rest of the week. I have to be at a Competition Commission hearing in Pretoria. I'll shower at the gym on my way home. Give me the number, I'll ask the plumber to come on Saturday.'

'Nonsense. Bring me your keys when you leave in the morning. I'll get my chap to come and sort it out.'

I'm too tired to argue.

*** * ***

I clutch a bag with a continental pillow under each arm and pick up two fistfuls of shopping bags. I'm about to step over the threshold when Dorothy's door opens. She does this all the time; I think she waits in her passage, listening for the sound of the key in my door.

I don't mind. Gogo would call a neighbour like her a godsend. The plumber came and went without me setting eyes on him. A new geyser was installed and tiles were replaced while I sweated to keep up at the Competition Commission hearing. Dorothy collected online quotes for household insurance and emailed them to me.

Her voice cracks through the small gap in her door. 'Hello lovey. Can you pop round for a minute?'

'Give me a minute, Dorothy,' I call out. 'Let me get my stuff inside.'

I plunk the bags down on the kitchen floor. Shopping used to be fun. When it's all you do every weekend it's torture. Why did nobody warn me that setting up a home was such hard work? I'm in no hurry to unpack. I'll get to it after I find out what Dorothy wants. Come to think of it, I haven't seen her for a day or two.

Her door is open. I knock and walk in. She's crouched on the plastic chair in front of her computer; her arms wrapped around her shins and her fingers laced together tight above her crossed ankles. Her eyebrows are painted on with thick black pencil and her lips look soaked in the red cochineal Gogo used for coconut ice. Dorothy looks scared. And a bit scary.

I put my hand on her shoulder. 'What's wrong?'

'There's something wrong. There's someone here.'

I don't get what she's saying. 'Who's here? What's wrong?'

Dorothy sniffs. 'I can smell someone was here. Maybe still is here.'

'Did you call security to take a look?'

She nods, her chin bouncing on knees locked tight together.

'Want me to check?'

Dorothy's bedroom is the same size as mine. Like her lounge, it's very short on furniture – there's a bed and nothing else. I open the built-in cupboards lining one wall. About ten hangers and two shelves hold all her clothing. Her spare bedroom is empty and so is its cupboard. There's no one in her shower or her broom cupboard. Her balcony's bare.

'There's only me and you here,' I report back.

Dorothy looks sick. The navy-blue skin under her eyes is pasted onto her cheekbones. I make her a mug of sweet tea, Gogo's cure for everything, and stay with her until she calms down a little.

I forgot about my shopping. The ice cream's melted. It's been stuffed into a bag with ten other things that need rinsing. Finally, I fall onto my deckchair on the balcony. There's a cup of coffee at my side and a Dunhill menthol shrinking between my fingers.

How freaky is Dorothy? It was strange, going through her things like that. Even stranger when I realized how little she had. There's something familiar about her, but I don't think we've met. She's unforgettable; most of her clothes are pink and white and that just looks wrong with white hair. She's quick to shift conversations back to me, I should pay more attention.

I deserve a break after the day I've had. I'm never going shopping at the Sandton mall on pay-day weekend again. I thought people this side of town would be different from my old neighbours in Soweto; that they would be stay-at-home-mummies who shopped on weekdays. I was so wrong; the mummies were all at the mall today with their aggressive husbands and their crying children.

Dorothy's balcony door slides open and cuts my break short. Can't the woman leave me alone for a few minutes? I've had enough of her madness for one day, I'm tired.

Her clown face smiles at me. 'Guess what? I found out what it was. I couldn't bear the thought of tossing and turning for another night so I went to investigate and I found out where the smell was coming from.'

I make her wait. I pull on my cigarette, hold and exhale a stream of smoke. 'So? Where?'

Dorothy digs a finger between the teabag titties on her chest. 'Me. The smell was coming from me. I checked everything and found out that the hypermarket had messed up my last delivery. They brought the wrong deodorant. It's the same brand I usually get; but the scent is different. It smells of musk, like a man.'

I can't believe I'm at the shops again. Dorothy says she won't be able to sleep tonight if she doesn't remove the smell from her body. She doesn't drive but, still, she could have come with me so that I don't have to fight for parking – again.

✳ ✳ ✳

I'm too skint to invite my chommas to my new home; too embarrassed to serve them nothing when they come. The iMac I planned to buy three months ago will have to wait a while longer. The housewarming comes first. I'm tired of being broke and lonely. Facebook friendships are no substitute for the real thing. I want to see faces crinkling up when my friends laugh at my jokes.

Tonight I don't want to be alone. I'm at Dorothy's door with a bottle of cheap rosé wine. I lift it above my head and speak in a dramatic voice when she opens. 'I have an announcement to make.'

I refuse to answer questions until I pour the wine and settle Dorothy in her chair. I lift my glass to my chest and stretch out my toast to myself; the news is too huge to tell in a rush.

'You... are in the company... of a lawyer... who was on the team... that just secured... the biggest merger ever... in all of South Africa's history!' I can't hold it in any longer. 'The Competition Commission said yes to an eight-billion-rand merger. I only played a small role, of course. They were already working on it when I joined the firm four months ago.'

Dorothy lifts her glass and sips from it like a baby bird. She puts it down and claps her hands, holding them sideways so there's little force and sound. 'Congratulations, my dear. That's marvellous.'

'Isn't it?' I smile proudly at myself. 'We had a press conference in our boardroom. They're streaming footage of it on *Business Day*'s website. Let me show you, there's about five seconds of my face, smiling like a fool.'

My fingers freeze on her iMac's mouse when I hear the disapproval, sharp as a reprimanding judge, in her voice.

'Leave it! Don't you dare load a newspaper site onto my computer.'

I turn with a smile. 'I don't have to bookmark it on your desktop. Let's just look at the footage. I want to show you, I'm famous.'

She's at my side, gripping my wrist. Her brown-spotted fingers are tougher than they look. This is weird. Why doesn't she want to see the footage? I thought I was internet savvy, but

Dorothy's taught me a thing or two. Her online community of handy men to fix things and shops that deliver sorted out half a page on my to-do list.

Why did she have to put me down like that? I try to keep my lip in while I speak, but it's hard. 'I came here to celebrate something important with you. Why did you have to spoil it?'

Dorothy's lips are pulled tight over her teeth. 'Don't you take that tone with me, young lady! The only one around here who's spoiled is you!'

If I say something, I'm going to get into trouble. What about you, I want to ask. Look how you live; there's a whole army of people fetching and bringing for you. You don't have to set foot outside. You send emails to my BlackBerry most days; asking me to stop at the shops on my way home from work.

I turn my back on her and walk to the door. I'm about to slam it behind me when I realize that I've left my wine behind. I'm not done with it yet.

Dorothy's at her computer when I get back into her lounge, watching something on her monitor. It's me. The camera mounted on the wall opposite her front door is pointed at my back. I move to the left and watch Dorothy appear. The resolution on the Mac is brilliant; we look like stars in a creepy film.

'That's how you know when I get home. You've been spying on me!'

Dorothy clicks on the mouse, shuts down the computer and twists around to face me. What is she expecting me to do? She's looking at me like a scared child who knows what's coming but doesn't have the nerve to run for safety.

I grab the bottle and close her door gently behind me as I leave.

✳ ✳ ✳

I stare at Dorothy's door as I walk up the steps to our shared landing. I miss her. I don't know why I freaked out so badly two weeks ago. She's not that strange. Okay, the fact that she never goes out; that's strange. I don't know if I can blame her, though. Joburg's streets are a war zone for women and she's a soft target in those little-girl outfits.

She's very organized despite her problem. The security camera was on the landing when I moved in; I just didn't know it was hooked up to her Mac. The camera's pointing at Dorothy's door. It doesn't move when I cross the landing to mine. I take four steps back, smile and wave. It watches me silently.

I march straight to the kitchen and put my briefcase on the counter. I'm starving. I had a meeting at eleven o'clock that went on through lunch and another one at three.

'Alone again tonight,' I complain to the African Violets. Their cheerful purple faces lift my mood, a little.

I have leftovers. I made my favourite last night: mutton curry. I lift the pot lid and inhale deeply; it's always better the next day when the spices are soaked into the meat. There's more than enough for two – I don't have to eat alone.

Dorothy's looking weird again when she opens her door. Her skin is bleached white enough to meet the high standards of Gogo's washing line. She isn't good company but it's better than eating alone. She hasn't said anything strange yet; she can't as long as she keeps shovelling food into her mouth like that. I'm about a third of my way through my meal when she hops off the barstool and out of the kitchen, muttering under her breath. I satisfy the worst of my hunger before I go find her.

Dorothy's at her computer, her back humped like a miner on his way home. She doesn't turn when I reach her side; her eyes are fixed on the monitor. She's staring at an exterior of a building lit up with harsh lights that turn everything into silhouettes. A car comes into view and I figure out what we're looking at: the security guard's office at the entrance to the complex. Dorothy must have another camera somewhere.

Her fingers move over the mouse and the image zooms towards the office window. I stare over her shoulder. There are two security guards inside, their black uniforms and skins indistinguishable in the dim light.

I keep my voice light. 'What are you looking at?'

She points at the screen with a long nail yellow at the tip. 'Them. They're both new, they arrived three days ago.'

I hadn't noticed new guards. I always wave in the direction of the office when I drive through the boom, picturing Emmanuel inside waving back at me. The small greeting makes me feel safe.

Dorothy leans forward, her face practically up against the monitor. 'They're huge. Nigerians maybe, or Congolese. What do you think?'

I step back. Crazy has started up again. It didn't take long to come. 'You can't tell what people are by looking at them.'

'Yes you can. I prefer Malawians, they're usually skinny. I like Zimbabweans. They have such gentle names like Lovejoy and Loveness and Lovesomemore. Their mothers had such hopes for them; I've never come across a Lovetostealyourlawnmowerafteryougivemeapiecejob.'

Dorothy's smile is false; she's showing too many of her small, mealie-kernel teeth. It's not going to help. As soon as I get my jumbled words straight in my head I'm going to give her a piece of my mind.

She can see something's up. 'What's wrong, lovey?'

I'm surprised by the realization that comes tumbling out of my mouth. 'Don't call me that. Don't you ever call me lovey again. You've never called me by my name once, do you know that? What's my name? Say it!'

Dorothy looks silently up at me. Her eyes are pitch black in her paper-white face, sinking deeper as she tries to look the innocent.

'Say Lerato. Say it.'

'Le-ra-to.'

'Good. You know what it means?'

I pick up a small shake of her head.

'It means "love" in Sesotho.'

Dorothy takes her eyes off the monitor and turns to me. 'Why are you getting so worked up? That's exactly what I've been calling you, lovey. Your mother also had high hopes for you.'

I come the closest I've ever been to hitting an old lady. My hand wants to lift up; I distract it by folding my arms. I'm too worked up to find the right words to tell Dorothy how much I resent her attitude. These will have to do. 'My mother did have high hopes for me, and I'm going to live up to them. She brought me onto this earth to spread love; not hatred like you.'

I walk out of Dorothy's place, swearing that I will never set foot inside again.

I curl up on my bed, facebooking my friends about the nasty bitch next door. Most of them are tired of Dorothy stories, but some take note when I introduce a new element: her racism. It's left a nasty smear on my flesh.

I post on my page: 'There's nothing worse than people reaching out with their prejudices and expecting you to receive it gladly.'

Why do I always think of the right thing to say long after it's required?

✳ ✳ ✳

Dorothy's on my mind throughout the short drive home from work. She's been there all day, watching as I questioned myself about whether I overreacted last night. It is irritating when a white person doesn't bother to learn a new name, but that's no proof Dorothy's a racist. She's done so much for me since I moved in next door to her four months ago, what's that about?

Emmanuel is on duty when I get home tonight, standing at the boom gate. He smiles and waves as I drive towards him.

His smile broadens when I come to a stop. He has a holster on his hip, the gun inside as black as his uniform and his shining boots.

We greet before I start questioning him gently. He's worked at the complex for ten years; it was his first, and only job, in Joburg. He tells me there are two new guards. One, like him, is from Limpopo and the other is a Zimbabwean.

'Why do you ask, Madam?'

I feel uncomfortable with Emmanuel calling me Madam and I tell him so before I answer his question. 'Mrs Walker told me. She notices everything.'

Emmanuel has such an open face. I watch patiently as thoughts crisscross it. It makes his gun, inches away from my face, less of a threat.

'Who is Mrs Walker?'

'Next door to me, in unit number five.'

'That's Mrs Campbell. Yes, she sees everything, she has cameras. She's had a hard life, that one. When I first came here journalists were coming every day for her. Some are big liars, they will say they are visiting someone but next thing they are banging on her door.'

Now it's Emmanuel's turn to wait while I try to organize my thoughts. I can't do it here. There's a car hooting behind me.

I haven't solved the mystery by the time I settle myself on my bed and power up my laptop. I google Dorothy Campbell.

I suck in my breath and lift a hand to my mouth to keep it in when the first page of links appear. Of course I know her! I was planning to use Campbell vs The Minister of Safety and Security and others as a precedent last year. My client's assault – which gave me nightmares from the day I met her till long after I quit the practice in fear – was nowhere near as bad as the one Dorothy survived.

Dorothy was gang raped eight years ago. The evidence vanished out of a police safe and the case against the accused was dismissed. She brought a high-court application against the investigating officers; and the court ruled that they were, indeed, negligent. Her rapists were prosecuted and convicted six years later – after the Minister of Safety and Security exhausted all his appeals.

The case was juicy enough for one of the tabloids to ignore the prohibition against publishing the names of rape victims. A day later most of the newspapers, radio and television stations carried the story and photographs of Dorothy, using the excuse that someone else had started first. A year later Dorothy was back on a front page under the headline, 'Brave rape victim's reconstructive surgery'.

I do a few sums in my head and work out that the damages she was awarded against the government and the media will keep her going for years – if she continues living frugally.

I was 18 when Dorothy was in the news; old enough to resent Gogo's fear that I would be raped whenever I set foot out of the door. Gogo prayed for Dorothy and her Women's Circle at the church had a cake sale to contribute to her legal fund. Gogo had pored over the newspaper articles; urging me to use my law degree to help women like this one.

I set my laptop aside, close my eyes, and think about what I've done to Dorothy.

✽ ✽ ✽

It's been a week since I've seen Dorothy. I kneel down and place an African Violet on her doormat. There's no card.

Rehana Rossouw lives in Johannesburg, in the bosom of her loving family. She has been a journalist for 30 years and is currently executive editor at *Business Day*. She has submitted her first novel to examiners at the end of a Masters Degree in Creative Writing at the University of the Witwatersrand and is anxiously awaiting their response.

The Verge

Rachel Zadok

IN THE DESERT THERE IS NOWHERE TO HIDE. Marcel stuck her index finger into a bullet hole to steady herself. Uncanny how Andrew had brought up the Euphorbia story on this same stretch of road, increasing the urgency of her need so she could no longer contain it. If they hadn't come across the abandoned Chevy pick-up, she'd have had to do it in the open, screened only by the scattered foliage of pencil bush, scrubby grass and Andrew's willingness to look the other way.

The cramps began at the border, after immigration stamped their passports and they settled back into the plush leather seats of the rented 4x4. Andrew turned the key in the ignition without immediately depressing the clutch and the black beast jolted violently, throwing Marcel forward so that her forehead connected with the windscreen. The bump wasn't painful, but it shook her up.

'Drive straight ahead for the next 253 kilometres, then turn left.' The inbuilt navigation's soothing middle-class accent had a sulky undertone that implied there would be trouble if you chose not to go her way. On the seven-hour trip up from Cape Town, Marcel hadn't noticed how like Natalie the navigation sounded, but, once in Namibia, the system's inane commentary began to grate on her nerves.

'Can't you turn that damn thing off?' she snapped, after the third instruction in 30 kilometres to drive in a straight line. He gave her a quizzical look, and she shifted against the leather and crossed her legs. Andrew thumbed the buttons on the steering-wheel control console. The sound of his window sliding down was like a tiny fighter jet preparing for take-off. Heat blasted into the air-conditioned interior; the air felt chalky in her throat.

Dr Evans had told Marcel, during one 500-rand session, that successful relationships were 80-per-cent honesty and 20-per-cent illusion. Preserving the illusions kept romance alive. Marcel wished Andrew would just suck it up and feign olfactory failure. After five years of well-modulated moaning, it was the least he could do.

She might have been able to hold on until they reached the campsite's concrete ablution block if he hadn't said '*Euphorbia tirucalli*' the way he did right then, stressing the last two syllables as if calling forth the Hindu goddess of death. She'd been compiling a guest list for their fifth-anniversary celebration in her head when he said it.

'Poison pencil bush, latin name *Euphorbia tirucalli*. It's so toxic that if you burned the dried plant and inhaled the smoke, you'd die.' Andrew sniffed; he always did when he felt he'd dispensed an interesting fact and wanted to punctuate it.

Marcel bit her lip. Davy had told her the same story a decade ago when he'd taken her camping to Namibia. She knew the movie. Her line was supposed to be, *they look like tumbleweeds from Spaghetti Westerns*, delivered in Natalie's sulky tone.

'Hmm, fascinating,' she said, the pitch of her voice rising. Her sunglasses were on her head, holding her hair back. She lowered them to cover her eyes and squeezed her lids shut. She'd freak out if the next thing he said was *nothing so innocuous*.

'In the Nineties, a ranger came across an entire family that had made a campfire from dried pencil bush. By sunrise, they were all dead. Mom, dad, three kids. Poor bastards.'

The story was bullshit, at best an urban legend. Marcel hated Namibia, the whole fucking country, with its unpolluted light and super-sized sky, but she couldn't say no. He'd already booked and paid and mapped the route with red plastic drawing pins. The road trip was a gift, a surprise. 'No' had never been an option. Not with Andrew.

Marcel turned her head and stared out through the unopened passenger-side window at the scorched terrain. The horizon wavered, fluid, unstable. Dust, kicked up by the tyres, tinted the glass and bloodied the landscape. The fine particles would work their way under the disintegrating rubber seals of her Leica and jam the mechanism.

Marcel loved shooting on film like diehard academics prefer paper books. Holidays provided the perfect opportunity to indulge her passion. A trip to Namibia required a camera with the capacity to withstand hard knocks. The hardy German Leica Davy had given her was the perfect choice.

She'd squatted behind that pick-up on that trip too, gazing at the bullet-riddled hood through a wide-angle lens. The Chevy looked no more corroded now than the first time she'd seen it, though the cooling fan no longer rotated in the breeze, its eerie hum silenced. She supposed it was the arid climate. Marcel too, had staved off the ravages of time with a vigorous moisturising routine and a vegan diet. Daily trips to the gym had whittled away at the curvaceousness of her youth. At 36, she was the leanest she'd ever been. A dried-up husk. Funny that she'd once wanted to be like Natalie, and had wished her own round buttocks and full breasts away.

Marcel remembered vividly the reds and greens of the oxidized metal popping against the endless expanse of cerulean sky. She'd been so focused on finding the perfect f-stop to capture the colours, she hadn't noticed Davy and Natalie in the corner of her composition. Weeks later, in the solitude of her darkroom, she'd submerged the exposed photographic paper in the developing bath and, as their ghostly forms solidified, fingers intertwined in a snatched moment of intimacy, she'd realized. Things between them must have begun before the trip.

When she'd returned to Cape Town, battered and bruised,

her feet blistered, she'd googled the Euphorbia story. There was no record of it on the internet. The lie had made her rage resurface, and she'd punched Davy's number into her keypad.

'This is Davy's phone, leave a message and I'll give it to him as soon as I can.' She'd listened to her peppy delivery of his voicemail, then hung up.

'I want my voicemail message to sound like the kind of secretary you can bend over the desk and spank,' he'd told her. They'd been out that night to see the movie with James Spader about a secretary who likes to cut herself, and were lying tangled in Davy's bed, his semen sticky between her legs. She'd thought he was the one, with his coppery skin and pale green eyes that seemed to question her soul every time he looked at her. Perhaps he was.

The next morning, Marcel loaded the Leica with a roll of vintage 35mm, and wandered into the bush to see if she could find a sociable weaver's nest. Two weavers had come to bathe in a puddle at the base of their campsite's tap. There had to be a nest nearby. The birds fascinated her, hundreds of them living together in the avian equivalent of a council estate.

Davy had told her that the largest colony ever discovered contained 5,732 birds. She'd been foolish to believe that, but she was only 26 then, and she'd have swallowed anything he'd asked her to. They'd pulled over to picnic, clearing a patch of ground under a camel thorn to lay their blanket. The tree contained a large nest and looked suffocated by a haystack. The discussion over a lunch of canned tuna and white bread, the only kind to be found in Namibia, had centred around the birds and had naturally progressed to communism.

'The weavers seem so cheerful,' Natalie had twittered. 'We could all learn a lesson about harmonious living from them, instead of being cranky just because three people have to share a tent.'

Davy had squeezed Marcel's thigh. She'd bitten her tongue for his sake but, that evening while Natalie showered, she'd told him what she thought of his new roommate. Who goes camping and forgets to bring a tent?

'So, she's a bit scatty, that doesn't equate to a low IQ.' Davy had gone on to point out that Natalie had come to Cape Town to write a dissertation on recovering from trauma in post-Apartheid South Africa. That he had defended her should have set alarm bells ringing, but Marcel had read the disappointment in his soul-searching eyes and felt chastised. She didn't have a degree, who was she to call someone stupid?

5,732 birds. The exactness of the number should have made her suspicious.

Marcel angled her lens at a dead ironwood and zoomed into the fingering branches. Black and blue filled her eye. She lowered the lens so she could see the eggshell pattern of the dry riverbed at the bottom of the composition, and depressed the shutter. She hoped the stark contrasts might produce an interesting effect. Expired film was unpredictable, the decades-old Kodak especially so. When she did manage to pull an image from the decayed silver halide, it was spectral, otherworldly, as if the emulsion was ectoplasmic and her camera a window to another dimension.

Marcel found the box of canisters in Munroes, displayed in a glass cabinet with some ancient Hasselblads. By the time her father had placed her first camera in her hands, age seven, Kodak came in black plastic. Mrs Munroe, the old witch, pretended she didn't want to sell, but in the end she let the box go for 200 bucks. Marcel could not believe her luck; most of the canisters had never been opened.

When she returned from her excursion, Andrew had struck camp and was waiting in the driver's seat with the engine purring. Bob Marley spilled from the open window, and his hand tapped out the rhythm against the door. She slowed her pace. Whenever they had to go to one of his dull faculty parties, he'd wait in the driveway while she dressed, depressing the hooter every five minutes as if he had a direct line from Telkom's 1-0-2-3 into his brain.

'At the sound of the tone, it will be five past six.' *Paaarp*.

She hated those parties, hated the way she was expected to stick on a smile and nod as if she understood String Theory and Occam's Razor, widening her eyes to feign interest and stop her brow from creasing. On Dr Evans' advice, Marcel made vision boards to help her realize her goals, but she never told him about the collage of facial features she'd cut from a fashion magazine and stuck on the inside of her wardrobe door. She took her time applying her lipstick and curling her lashes just so, that mask her only defence against Andrew's dowdy academic-supernova friends.

Marcel climbed into the 4x4 and buckled her seatbelt. Dr Evans said that guilt was the least useful emotion. Rage you could channel, but guilt ate you from the inside. As they pulled off, she cut a sideways glance at Andrew to gauge his mood. He was staring straight ahead, lips sucked in. His scalp looked angry. A model wife would have offered to rub Aloe Vera gel into his sunburn, but she could not bring herself to sink her fingertips into his thinning hair.

'Are you ready to see the largest fissure in Africa?' Andrew reversed the 4x4 into a parking spot at one of the official look-out points. He turned to her, baring his teeth in a facsimile of a smile. A lump of breakfast clawed up her gullet into her mouth. She swallowed audibly. If anyone were to drag her to this godforsaken hole again, she'd bring a loaf of rye.

Andrew walked around the 4x4 and opened Marcel's door. She stepped out reluctantly and, though there wasn't another soul around, he aimed the remote. There was blip-blip as the vehicle locked.

'Baboons,' he offered by way of explanation, 'you can't be too careful.' He handed Marcel the keys to stow in her camera bag, and strode to the rim of the canyon.

'At 160 kilometres long and 550 metres deep, the Fish

River Canyon is the second largest in the world. Spectacular, don't you agree?'

Marcel gazed into the ravine, dizzy with vertigo. It was as if some gigantic being had stuck their hands into the earth and ripped it apart. Aloes the raw colour of scald wounds clung to the cliffs. There was no other vegetation to stabilize the shale. Once you were in, you couldn't get out.

Andrew draped his arm over her shoulders. 'It takes two hours to hike to the bottom. 550 metres. That's more than half a kilometre, honey.'

She shrugged him off. 'Believe it or not, Andrew, I know how many metres make up a kilometre.'

He blinked, colourless lashes flickering. 'Jesus, Marcel, what's gotten into you. You've been very bitchy since we left Cape Town. I don't quite know how to deal with this new you.'

She watched him stalk away, then clicked the lens cap off the Leica and stared through the viewfinder into the chasm.

The canyon had been closed to hikers for three weeks in anticipation of the summer rains when they descended into it; Davy taking the lead with Marcel bringing up the rear, Natalie between them. They could not risk making their entry on the official trail near Hobas, and had to zigzag illegally along the ridges. The soles of their hiking boots set off mini-avalanches of shale. Progress was incremental. At midday, they were forced to take shelter from the blazing sun in a slim crescent of shade cast by a boulder. After two hours of walking, they were halfway, suspended between riverbed and sky.

'This is crazy, guys. Seriously, we should turn back.'

'There's only one way out of here now.' Davy gave her a lunatic grin. They were doomed, Marcel could feel it. Five days hiking through a canyon on the brink of flooding. She should have made more of an effort to talk him out of it, but Natalie had said yes.

When they finally reached the bottom, Davy's excitement

whooped out of him and bounced off the canyon walls. Marcel dropped her pack and sank to her knees. She watched Natalie turn cartwheels, then flip onto her hands, pointing her boots to the sky. Her tank top slid over her head, exposing her prepubescent-sized breasts, nipples the colour of unripe watermelon. Davy watched her too, the tip of his tongue poking from the corner of his mouth.

The light was receding rapidly, shading the riverbed in lilacs and purples. Davy and Natalie went off to find something to burn while Marcel set up a basic camp. She unrolled their sleeping bags, assembled the small gas camping stove. Then she sat in the darkening canyon, staring up at the sharp angle the dwindling sunlight cut across the rocks until it disappeared. The silence bore down on her, as if trying to get in. When Davy and Natalie returned, skin flushed as if the exertion of their descent had not yet worn off, she was shivering.

'What took so long? You've been gone ages.'

Davy shrugged, and dropped a bundle of sticks at her feet. He pulled her close and pressed his mouth to her. His lips felt raw, his saliva left a musky taste on her tongue.

As a child, her father had told her that one ostrich yolk was equivalent to 24 chicken yolks. The next day, standing in front of her class holding an ostrich egg aloft, she'd garbled the fact. Everyone laughed, even the teacher, but she'd not known why. Marcel felt that same confusion when Davy kissed her.

On the third morning in the canyon, Marcel watched Davy lift Natalie's pink nylon backpack onto her shoulders and secure the belt at her hips. His hands slid upwards and lingered at her waist. Natalie leaned into him and gave Marcel a knowing smile, the kind two people sharing a private joke give each other over the table at stuffy dinner parties.

Marcel ran then, the echoes of her enraged *fuck you* tailgating her pounding feet. She wanted to escape, sprint all the way to the exit point at Ais Ais without stopping, but in the end, her breath defeated her. She clambered onto a large boulder to wait.

They appeared 20 minutes later, strolling along as if nothing was amiss. When they reached the boulder, they squinted up at her, wearing matching madcap grins. Natalie dropped her pack, climbed up next to Marcel, and draped an arm over her shoulder. They sat for a full minute, saying nothing. Then she'd pressed her lips to Marcel's cheek and nibbled a path to her ear.

'I don't mind sharing if you don't,' she whispered.

The hollowness inside Marcel expanded, thinning her skin so that the vast silence penetrated her. She placed her hands on Natalie's waist, held her sulky blue gaze. Then she gave her a knowing smile and a hard shove.

The first time Marcel loaded a roll of the Kodak into her Leica, she'd pointed the lens at a random stranger sitting at a café across the street from her flat, and seen him, bent over a sheaf of papers with an intense expression. She stared at him through the lens, focusing, blurring, focusing; the sandy shoulder-length hair, the strong jaw shadowed by stubble. After four years of radio silence, she needed to speak to him. She shotgunned another tumbler of the whiskey and crossed the road.

'Hey, long time.' Made brave by alcohol, she pulled out the chair opposite at him and sat down. He frowned at her, no glimmer of recognition in his flat green eyes. She felt like she'd been punched in the chest. Three months was not long term, she knew, but their entanglement had been so intense she'd been unable to feel anything since. How could he not remember her?

'I'm sorry, do I know you?'

Through a haze of alcohol, she squinted at the smattering of freckles marching across his aquiline nose. Her tears had come then, hot and fast, blobbing the ink on his papers. His hand darted across the table to rescue the student essay.

'Look, I don't know you, but if you want to talk about something... my name's Andrew and I'm a pretty good listener.'

'What?' she'd sniffed.

'I counsel my students all the time. Whatever ails you, I've heard it before.' He grasped her hand and gazed at her with Dr Evans earnestness. She eyed the blunt edges of his nails, the blond, almost transparent hair between the knuckles of his delicate piano-playing fingers, and knew she could never describe the sound of a skull smashing against rock to someone so clean.

The last time she saw Davy was at a prayer service for Natalie. She read the announcement in the newspaper and had gone to the chapel at UCT because she knew he would be there. She sought him out in the crowd, and they stood side by side in conspiratorial silence while the dean spoke of how saddened he was to live in a country where a student with so much promise could just disappear. Marcel wondered whether failing students were mourned by so many.

There had been no signal at the bottom of the canyon, no way to call a rescue team to airlift Natalie and her broken head to safety. It was two days' walk to Ais Ais and, as slight as Natalie was, they could not carry her out. Marcel dragged her body to a pool of water where it was sure to be subsumed by the flood, and then she took Davy by the hand and led him out of the canyon.

Marcel found Andrew standing on a precipice, watching an eagle through binoculars. She placed her hands between his shoulder blades, and massaged the ridges of his spine with the heel of her palm.

'I have a surprise for you,' he said. 'Something that may cheer you up. I've hired a guide to take us hiking. I've packed everything we need. We'll spend tonight in Hobas, but tomorrow night we'll sleep at the bottom of the Fish River Canyon.'

The face peering down at her had the pale kind of skin that didn't like sun. He would never glow with burnished light as if the pure essence of him could not be contained by his flesh.

'Excited, darling?'

Marcel smiled at him as if they were sharing their first private joke. Then she gave him a hard shove. He dropped silently into the canyon unable, without textbook guidance, to express his unexpected death.

If Dr Evans asked her why, she might tell him divorce was too messy for someone who lined his marking pencils at right angles to the edge of his polished oak desk and stacked his student's essays like brand-new reams of Typec. But Dr Evans need never know. Relationships were 80-per-cent honesty and 20-per-cent illusion. Marcel snapped the cap onto her lens and walked back to the 4x4.

Rachel Zadok is the author of *Gem Squash Tokoloshe* (shortlisted for the Whitbread First Novel Award and the John Llewellyn Rhys Prize). She is the organizer of Short Story Day South and lives in Cape Town.

Rules

The prize is awarded annually to a short story by an African writer published in English, whether in Africa or elsewhere. (The indicative length is between 3,000 and 10,000 words.)

'An African writer' is normally taken to mean someone who was born in Africa, or who is a national of an African country, or whose parents are African.

There is a cash prize of £10,000 for the winning author and a travel award for each of the shortlisted candidates (up to five in all).

For practical reasons, unpublished work and work in other languages is not eligible. Works translated into English from other languages are not excluded, provided they have been published in translation and, should such a work win, a proportion of the prize would be awarded to the translator.

The award is made in July each year, the deadline for submissions being 31 January. The shortlist is selected from work published in the five years preceding the submissions deadline and not previously considered for a Caine Prize. Submissions, including those from online journals, should be made by publishers and will need to be accompanied by six original published copies of the work for consideration, sent to the address below. There is no application form.

Every effort is made to publicize the work of the shortlisted authors through the broadcast as well as the printed media.

Winning and shortlisted authors will be invited to participate in writers' workshops in Africa and elsewhere as resources permit.

The above rules were designed essentially to launch the Caine Prize and may be modified in the light of experience. Their objective is to establish the Caine Prize as a benchmark for excellence in African writing.

The Caine Prize
The Menier Gallery
Menier Chocolate Factory
51 Southwark Street
London, SE1 1RU, UK
Telephone: +44 (0)20 7378 6234
Email: info@caineprize.com
Website: www.caineprize.com